A Pictorial History
of the Carousel

A PICTORIAL HISTORY OF THE

CAROUSEL

FREDERICK FRIED

South Brunswick and New York: A. S. Barnes and Company
London: Thomas Yoseloff Ltd

© MCMLXIV by A. S. Barnes and Company, Inc.
Library of Congress Catalogue Card Number: 64–17409

Printed in the United States of America

A. S. Barnes and Co., Inc.
Cranbury, New Jersey 08512

Thomas Yoseloff Ltd
Magdalen House
136-148 Tooley Street
London SE1 2TT, England

REISSUED 1978

ISBN 0-498-06170-1

TO BOBBY AND RACHEL

CONTENTS

CHAPTER 1

THE EVOLUTION OF
THE CAROUSEL

CAROUSELS HAVE BEEN KNOWN BY MANY NAMES. IN ENGLAND, THEY HAVE BEEN CALLED THE roundabouts, gallopers, or tilts; in France, *caroussels* and *manèges de chevaux de bois* (a riding ring of wooden horses); in Holland, *stoomcaroussel;* *torneo* in Italy; *karussel* in Germany. In America, we have had many names also: flying horses, whirligig, flying Dutchmen, flying jinny, Kelly's goats, spinning jinny, hobby horses, steam circus, steam riding galleries, galloping-horse steam carousels, carry-us-alls, and of course, merry-go-rounds.

No one can say with assurance just where or when the first carousel appeared. The earliest visual record of a carousel device appears in a Byzantine bas-relief 1500 years ago. Later, travelers from abroad brought back stories and sketches of such devices. One water color depicting a fair from the early seventeenth century shows two variations of Turkish merry-go-rounds, as well as a Ferris wheel, swings, and other amusements.

One description of an early carousel device (published by the Hakluyt Society) in *The Travels of Peter Mundy in Europe and Asia 1608–1667*, states that in 1620:

We came to the cittie of Philippopolis [Bulgaria] . . . One [carousel] is like a crane wheel . . . and turned in that manner, whereon, children sit on little seats hung around in several parts thereof, and though it turns right up and down, and that the children are some times on the upper part of the wheel, and some times on the lower, yet they always sit upright . . . another is like a great cart wheel, on whose circumference are fastened little seats, whereon the children being sat, the wheel is put about, they all going around horizontal-wise . . .

In countries as remote as Mexico and India, a strange form of the carousel was in use. The Aztecs had a ceremony in which natives, dressed in the plumage of birds of prey, hung by their heels, head downward, suspended by ropes from an eighty-foot pole. The rope was wound tightly around a tree, and when it unwound, it sent the flyers outward, horizontal to the ground, spinning at great speeds. A terrifying and bloody spectacle, it is practiced

13

Byzantine bas-relief, *ca.* 500 A.D. Acrobats, jugglers, bears, and spectators watch the riders swinging in baskets tied to a centerpole. (*Deutsches Bildarchive*)

Early seventeenth-century water color. A carousel (*upper right*) is one of the features of this fairground. The riders, armed with sticks, are trying to knock the hat off the man standing nearby. At another carousel (*center left*) a man stands on a platform and turns the ride by hand. (*Picture Collection, New York Public Library*)

Fifteenth-century drawing of a carousel (found in a manuscript). The man in the tall hat is armed, and the riders attempt to kick off his hat. This carousel embodies the principles of the wheel, the centerpole—and manpower.

"The Game of Flyers," played in ancient Mexico. (*Picture Collection, New York Public Library*)

A sketch of the carousel at Philippopolis as it is described in *The Travels of Peter Mundy, 1608–1667.*

Carousel flying in India. (*Picture Collection, New York Public Library*)

Le Grand Carrousel de 1662.

even to this day. They called it "The Game of the Flyers." But in India, carousel flying was a harmless sport engaged in at festivals of supplication and attended by Maharajahs and their mahouts, servants, and soldiers.

While the actual origin of the carousel is unknown, and although it may have developed independently in several parts of the world, it is known that the word "carousel" derives from the ancient Italian and Spanish words *garosello* or *carosella* meaning "little war." This name describes what was at first a serious game played by horsemen in Arabia and Turkey during the twelfth century.

Little clay balls filled with scented water were used by these horsemen and thrown to each other—the object was not to miss the catch. This game caught the attention of the Italian and Spanish crusaders who brought it back to Europe. The Italian pages of Charles VIII introduced it to France about the time Columbus was discovering America. The French called the game *carrousel* and changed its character into a lavish display of raiment and horsemanship. The first of these French *carrousels* occurred during the reign of Henry of Navarre (1553–1610), and the most famous one took place on June 5 and 6, 1662. It was a great spectacle given by Henry's grandson, Louis XIV, to impress his teen-age mistress, Louise de la Vallière. It was staged in the square between the Tuileries and the Louvre. This area is still called the "Place du Carrousel," and the "Arc du Carrousel" is a tourist attraction to this day.

18

For this grand event, the costumers, *couturiers*, wigmakers, saddlers, and others were all engaged in their own tournament to outdesign each other. Mythology and history were overtaxed for new creations and months were spent in the execution of the costumes. The whole court took part in this grand event and even Voltaire was moved to write a treatise on its magnificence. Costing 1,200,000 livres, a stupendous sum for even these times, it turned out to be more of a daylight fancy ball on horseback than a "little war." In a setting of blasting trumpets and brilliant fluttering pennons there was the ball game in which brightly colored balls were tossed at the participants, perfuming the "enemy." The wind would waft the scent to the sidelines filled with spectators, and everyone would sniff approvingly, identifying their side by the fragrance. Everyone, except the peasantry, had a delightful time.

Frederick II of Prussia in 1750, in Berlin, also had a huge attendance for his *carrousel;* in Russia, the Countess Orlov sponsored a private tournament as late as 1811. Today in Saumur, France, The *Carrousel* of the Black Squadron is held each year by the cadets from the Academy, continuing the tradition of the seventeenth century.

One important aspect of the *carrousel* was the ring-spearing tournament. The Moors are considered the originators of this sport, and from Spain it found its way all through Europe. In thirteenth-century England this game was known as "Tilting at the Quintain," derived from the Italian *Correre alla Quintana*. It required a steady lance, great horsemanship, and a keen eye. The object was to lance the ring suspended on brightly colored ribbons from a limb of a tree or between two posts. When lanced, the ring slid down the shaft and a stream of ribbons fluttered in the wind. Sometimes, the lancer rode in a chariot, reins in one hand, lance in the other.

This same contest was popular in many lands and until recently in many rural regions of the United States. An engraving appearing in *Gleason's Pictorial* of 1851 shows our American knights in this non-combative form of jousting.

In France about 1680, the carousel became mechanical. Someone thought of suspending horses and chariots by chains from arms radiating from a centerpole. A horse, mule, or man supplied the motive power and the carousel became a device for training young nobility for the tournament of ring spearing. In a sketch from Holland of the seventeenth century, we see the horse as the motive power.

Although Dr. Samuel Johnson did not think it important to mention it in his dictionary, the earliest use of the term "merry-go-round" for carousel is found in a poem by George Alexander Stevens (published in 1729) describing the St. Bartholomew Fair in England:

> Here's Whittington's cat and the tall dromedary,
> The chaise without horses, and Queen of Hungary:
> Here's the merry-go-rounds, come who rides, come who rides, Sir?
> Wine, beer and cakes, fire eating besides, Sir;
> The fam'd learned dog that can tell all his letters,
> And some men, as scholars, are not much his betters.

Engraved by Jean Papillon in 1766, a symbolic French carousel allegorically represents the ring game. Two heavy planks, assembled to form a cross, turn on an axle placed into the center of a mill composed of four wooden beams joined one to another by cross pieces supported by consoles. At the end of each of the planks, two chariots pulled by dragons and two cavaliers astride noble chargers are symmetrically placed. Each holds a long wooden tournament lance. The ring is suspended from a little gibbet crowned with a fleur-de-lis. The tilters can test their skill on a shield, a helmet, or a head. At the junction are four allegorical figures representing the seasons. In the foreground is Summer with a sheaf of wheat and Autumn with a garland of grape vine and a wine cup. At the top of the central post is a winged victory proclaiming the glory of the winner of the game.

19

Escadron des Turcs. Many of the decorations and trappings used on later merry-go-round horses were influenced by pictures of the *Turcs* commanded by the Prince de Condé in *Le Grand Carrousel de 1662.*

Tilting for the ring. Here we see the penalty for an unsteady hand. (*Picture Collection, New York Public Library*)

French carousel, 1680.

American Grand Tournament scene, *Gleason's Pictorial,* 1851.

Saint Bartholomew Fair, 1728. The mechanism is an early version of the Ferris wheel, known as "Ups and Downs." The artist omitted the fourth stall in order to show the workings of the wheel, and he also denied legs to the drinker.

A drawing of an eighteenth-century English carousel. As we can see, the lines by J. Beresford in his *Miseries of Human Life* (London, 1807), "May she fall to the ground from a merry-go-round," described a real danger.

Le jeu de Bague de Jean Papillon, 1766.

Le Jardin de Monceau near Paris, 1779.

In France, as begun in the seventeenth century, the carousel became an important source of entertainment, and in 1779, a carousel was erected on the grounds of His Most Serene Highness, Monseigneur the Duke of Chartres. Monceau Gardens, now known as Parc Monceau, near Paris, was the site of this unusual carousel. In the park was a small artificial lake with faked ruins of a colonnade and the actual ruins of antique temples (which exist today). A description from the period follows:

In front of the building is a pond encircling the carousel, thereby closing it off as an island. The carousel consists of a Chinese parasol with three supports. It turns by footwork on a treadmill at the center. From the rim of the platform extend four iron bars, two are dragons, mounted by male riders, the other two support attendants dressed as Chinese crouched on their sides. Across one arm they carry a pillow for the ladies to sit upon, the other arm holds a pillow for the rider's feet. The ladies carry tassled parasols with little bells. The border of the large parasol is decorated with ostrich eggs and small bells. Four lanterns (seen in the illustration) contain rings which are released by pulling on the tassel at the base of the lantern.

The Duke de Chartres, also called Phillipe Égalité, a friend of the revolution, was beheaded ten years later. Perhaps this delightful extravagance was a contributory factor.

In 1798 another French variation of the carousel developed wheels, an exciting innovation at this time, but strangely, they were omitted on future rides but show up again one hundred years later on American Tonawanda merry-go-rounds.

24

Fig. 1.

Fig. 2.

French carousel, three views, 1789.

25

Le Jeu de Bague dans une Fête Publique, 1779. While the nobility amused itself on a more elaborate scale, the public was invited (for a sou) to ride on more crude machines. The horses had no legs, and the power was supplied by a boy. (*Picture Collection, New York Public Library*)

Le Amusements de la Bague Chinoise au Jardin de Tivoli

Frontispiece for *L'Ami des Enfans*, Paris, 1803. (*Picture Collection, New York Public Library*)

La Flotte Aérienne, published in the journal *La Caricature*, 1832.

Le Vélocipède-Carrousel, Invention Américaine, 1869.

Duc Orléans *et le Deux Princesses.* **French satire on politics. While the personages are turning swiftly, one sees King Louis-Philippe pushing, with much suffering, the entire ring. The master of the game, releasing the rings down the slide, is Minister Tallyrand who negotiated the marriage for the Duke of Orleans, who is trying to steal a ring with his sword; the princesses are far off, with rings on their fingers and thumbs to their noses.** (*Picture Collection, New York Public Library*)

Drawing by George Cruickshank in 1822 used as the frontispiece for *Life in Paris of Dick Wildlife* by David Carey.

A Paris sketch of the Champs Élysées, *Harpers*, 1874.

Another political cartoon, 1848 (the horses have been perfected and are now equipped with legs). The characters are: Prince Louis Bonaparte, Cavaignac, Ledru-Rollin, Lamartine, Raspail, and Marest. Some are symbolized by an emblem —the eagle, the lyre, the apothecary jar of camphor. The Prince of Joinville and Louis Blanc are turning the ride. Each rider is trying to spear the most electoral votes for the presidency of the Republic.

During the Restoration in 1815, carousels continued to be a source of pleasure and amusement. In another version, entitled "The Chinese Ring Game in the Tivoli Garden," from the *Non Genre* series, a stately lady released little rings as the riders gaily tried to spear them with their miniature lances. But it was no fun for the man in the pit trudging around in dizzying circles, turning the ride.

About 1832, a new method for turning the carousel was introduced. A man stood at the centerpole and cranked a handle. By a set of gears attached to the worm gear in the center shaft, the carousel was made to spin. The faster the cranking action the greater the speed. Simultaneously, one appeared in England and another in France. Balloon ascensions were popular about this period and the name given this new ride was "The Air-borne Fleet." A rocking action of the boats, simulating waves, with five big dips at each turn was accomplished by a double-pivoted bascule at the center, somewhat like a see-saw. We are left up in the air as to how the riders got in and out.

In the French *Brevets d'Inventions*, a M. Cardinet patented an ingenious variation of the carousel. In this invention, the wooden horses were actually set in motion by pedals serving as stirrups. The riders had to pedal conscientiously to make the machine turn. They certainly deserved all the fun they may have gotten from it. An American invention, called the *velocipède carrousel*, appeared in France in 1869 and its riders also merited their pleasures. (This ride was installed in Steeplechase, Brooklyn, at the turn of the century and is still in active use.)

By 1822 the carousel was such a popular and accessible form of entertainment that it had become a handy vehicle for satirists, political cartoonists, and humorists.

The French had provided the name, developed the carousels introduced by the Turks, and added the brass ring to the mechanical ride. They then brought it to the highest stage in which it could be driven by man or beast. It was the English who provided the tremendous stimulus which advanced the carousel into a new epoch.

30

CHAPTER 2

EUROPEAN CAROUSEL MAKERS

PRIOR TO 1860, THE CAROUSEL WAS LIMITED IN WEIGHT AND SIZE BECAUSE OF MOTIVE POWER. With the invention of the steam engine and its application as a driving force, a new impetus pushed the development of the carousel forward.

ENGLAND

About 1865, S. G. Soames of Marsham, England, applied steam as a driving power by using a stationary engine and a flat-belt drive. He called his machine the "Steam Circus." The name suggests that other animals as well as horses were used. (Horses, however, dominated the carousel and its variant forms.) Soames found the belt drive unsatisfactory, did not develop it any further, and finally abandoned it.

In 1858, Frederick Savage, a young machinist, exhibited his first road engine at the Long Sutton Show. Savage was born on March 3, 1828, in the Norfolk village of Hevinghas and at sixteen obtained employment in East Dereham with a whitesmith and machine maker, Thomas Cooper, who had a small foundry there. After four years, Savage moved to Kings Lynn and went to work in a small machine shop for Charles Willett. Not long after, Willett retired and Savage opened his own works. Contemporary records describe him as "Engineer & Agricultural Machinist."

About 1870, Frederick Savage mounted a small engine on wheels fitted a cog wheel, a crown wheel, and pinion wheel, all connected with a "cheese wheel" into which the radiating spars called "swifts" or "sweeps" were fitted. This became known as the "center truck."

A rotating frame, which supported various forms of carriages for riders, increased in size and this led to the three- and four-abreast carousels or roundabouts, as they were called, ranging from thirty-six feet to forty-eight feet in diameter. Frederick Savage also designed and patented the overhead cranking device that gave an up and down or jumping motion to the horses and is found on most carousels today. These became known as "gallopers" in England and "jumpers" in America.

Frederick Savage of Kings Lynn

The "center truck," 1870.

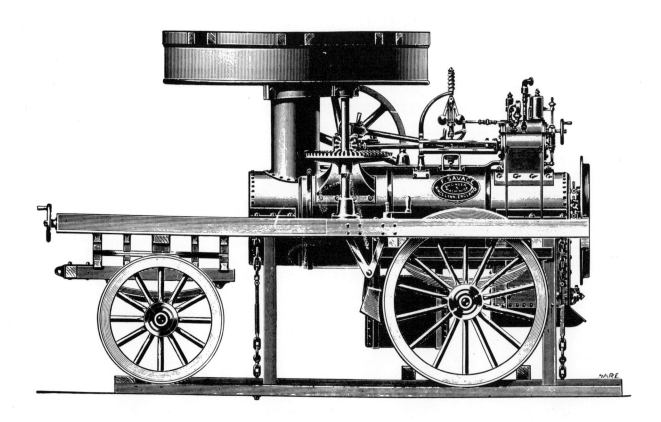

First platform set of horses built by Savage in England, *ca.* 1880 (owned by the late Patrick Collins). It bears a similarity to the construction of the American Tonawanda machines of a later date. (*Father P. R. Greville*)

"Rolling Gondolas" (owned by John Studt). Built by Savage and photographed in South Wales, 1896. (*William Keating*)

A second, lower platform was added, reached by one or two steps, to facilitate the loading and unloading of the riders. These machines had a fair amount of speed, and to counter the centrifugal force, which would tend to unseat the riders, the horse rods were extended to pass below the body of the horse and through the loading platform. This device, by a grooved slot, permitted the horses and riders to swing out some ten to fifteen degrees as the speed of the ride increased, enabling the riders to keep their seats with ease. In America, at a later date, this problem was solved by tilting the platform inward toward the center ¾ inch per foot, somewhat like modern highways.

With Savage's contributions, it was possible to place great weights on the carousel. Elaborately carved horses and animals of all kinds were added. Rounding boards which formed the upper, outer rim of the carousel were highly decorated, and in time, not an inch was left uncarved.

Early type switchback, photographed at Accrington, Lancashire, 1889. Extended centerpole is actually the smoke stack from the steam engine. (*William Keating*)

"Rolling Ships" (owned by G. Twigdon). Built by Savage and photographed at Derbyshire, 1885. (*William Keating*)

The roundabout became an elaborate showpiece and the firm of Frederick Savage became an outstanding maker of carousels and fairground machinery. Savage also made a type of carousel or roundabout called a "switchback." An early type switchback was made for the English showman John Green and is believed to date from 1880.

The switchback, a circular railroad consisting of eight riding-cars coupled together and driven around an undulating circular track, coursed over two hills and dales. In the center of the machine was the center engine mounted on a gauntry. All were balanced and spun from this central point. The cars were mounted on low wheels, had seats fixed across, and the riders all faced forward.

When the switchback was first introduced, there were only two rails. When the cars went uphill some were derailed, with unhappy results. This problem was soon solved by adding a third rail—big, little, and inside trams kept the cars truly on course. After this problem was solved, more elaborate designs appeared, such as Twigdon's "Rolling Ships" built by Savage and dated about 1885.

Development continued and the center pole became the chimney for the center engine. A canvas top was added as protection against the elements. Domes and droppers were fixed to the uprights and were rich in carving gilding, and color. All the working parts were encased by elaborate carvings which in time reached a highly specialized style of "fairground rococo." One of the early elaborate rides was Fred Hodder's "Rollings Ships," shown at Derbyshire in 1890 and built by Savage's Ltd at Kings Lynn.

34

"Rolling Ships" (owned by Fred Hodder), 1890. (*William Keating*)

"Scenic Railway" (owned by White Brothers). Built by Orton Sons and Spooner, Ltd., Cardiff, 1918.

Shortly after 1870, when Frederick Savage began the production of fairground machinery, his firm stated that "some hundreds of steam driven roundabouts, switchbacks, swings and other novelties left St. Nicholas works, all the wood carving and gilding necessary being carried out in the same premises by skilled tradesmen." By 1890 in England, the carving and decorating of roundabout and fairground equipment became a highly skilled business and several firms found steady employment in this trade.

Perhaps the best known of these firms was Orton Sons and Spooner Ltd at Burton-on-Trent. Crude cars gave way to elaborate Venetian gondolas, and with constant improvements, the wheels, now rubber encased, silently glided along. The roundabouts and other circular rides took on huge proportions. A massive "Scenic Railway," sixty feet in diameter and fifty-feet high was created by Orton Sons and Spooner for White Brothers at Cardiff. Each car weighed one ton ten cwts. (unloaded).

The English roundabout runs clockwise with no known exceptions. A horse is mounted on his left side, which is correct equestrian etiquette. The loading and unloading may have been the original factor. English horses are carved so that the flowing mane of the horse appears on his left or outward side. The left is also the more decorative and carved side. The inside horses were less carved and decorated and the innermost ones barely carved.

Dragon car "Scenic Railway" (owned by Enoch Farrar) and photographed at Grantham, Lincolnshire, 1920. Elaborate decoration made by Orton Sons and Spooner. (*William Keating*)

A disastrous fire at Wisbeck, Lincolnshire, 1926, left Enoch Farrar's Whale car "Scenic Railway" a blackened ruin. (*William Keating*)

Hereford May Fair, 1912. The grand "Fourabreast" (owned by John Studt) photographed in the rain. (*William Keating*)

"Four-abreast" gallopers (owned by Billy Butlin), Skegness, Lincolnshire. (*William Keating*)

"Grand Gondola" switchback (owned by George Green), photographed at Dumfries, Scotland, 1910.

White Brothers (Cardiff) four-abreast gallopers were undoubtedly the greatest and most magnificent roundabouts to be seen on British fairgrounds. The first model was built for John Studt of Cardiff in 1900 and in 1914 sold to White's, who later engaged Orton & Spooner to further elaborate the ride, particularly by making some spectacular, deep rounding-boards. This machine is now owned by Billy Butlin and is at Skegness Amusement Park (Lincolnshire), its center engine replaced by an electric motor and its organ silent.

Frederick Savage, elected Mayor of Kings Lynn from 1889–90 (as was his son later) died on April 27, 1897, leaving his business to his sons who reorganized the company under the name Savage Brothers Ltd. The firm is still in business and manufactures various types of machinery under the name, Savages, Ltd. Other English roundabout makers were R. J. Lakin and Co.; Lang Wheels; Maxwell, and also Anderson.

George Green's road locomotive. Built by William Foster and Company of Lincoln, photographed, 1909.

On the main Lincoln to Boston road, 1907. Part of Mrs. Annie Holland's Bioscope Show en route, drawn by the Burrell road locomotive, "Challenger." These engines, all with superlative names, are now rare objects, highly prized by collectors. (*William Keating*)

Many of these roundabouts, switchbacks, and scenic railways were constructed to be portable and, despite their huge weight and bulk, could be dismantled and erected again in a remarkably short period of time. It is a wonder how well many held up after hundreds of these knockdowns and setups. (An important part of the moving operation was the road locomotive or traction engine, constructed so that apart from hauling the trucks on the road, it also acted as a center engine.) However, the materials were so heavy that at least nine trucks were needed to transport the carousels and it became unprofitable.

About 1911 or 1912, electricity was first introduced as the motive power and the roundabout reached its full maturity. But many of the old roundabouts and switchbacks slowly disappeared from the fairgrounds. During World War II, the British Government, in order to boost morale, recommended their return and the old noble pleasure vehicles once more brought joy and happiness.

Annual Goose Fair at Nottingham, October 12, 1907. (*Picture Collection, New York Public Library*)

Die Amazone der Hasenhaide, 1850. Carousel in the Hasenhaide, an early amusement park in Berlin. The ladies who dared ride were called amazons.

Umbrella-top German *Karoussel*, 1850. Some German carousels went clockwise, like roundabouts, but in later years, all went counter-clockwise. The lancer on the wooden charger is set to spear a ring, entitling him to a free ride if successful.

'Chinese Ring Game," Tivoli Gardens, Paris, 1815. The source of power was the man in the pit.

Title page of promotion and instruction manual issued by Norman & Evans in 1898.

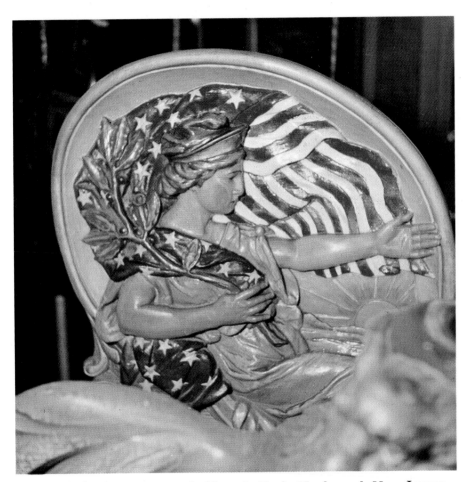

Carved chariot on carousel, Olympic Park, Maplewood, New Jersey.

Primitive giraffe (Swenson Collection).

Parker horse and Looff grey-hound (Swenson Collection on exhibition at Early American Folk Art Museum, New York City).

Roundabout dragon (Swenson Collection).

Lead horse, Dentzel's favorite carousel at Lambertville, New Jersey.

Detail showing upper outside rim and inside of Dentzel's favorite carousel at Lambertville, New Jersey, owned by the author.

Cat with fish, Dentzel's favorite carousel at Lambertville, New Jersey.

Detail of section, upper outside rim of Olympic Park Carousel, Maplewood, New Jersey.

Carousel horse, Olympic Park, Maplewood, New Jersey, carved by Daniel C. Muller for the Philadelphia Toboggan Company.

Today, many gallopers (as well as other carousel accoutrements), with their names brightly painted in brilliant colors and streamers on their chests or necks, can be found in the basements of New York antique dealers. One importer of antiques has a cellar full of fine old rounding-boards from several roundabouts that graced the best of the British fair grounds.

One of the greatest of all sights was one of the British fair grounds. Fairs are a very old tradition in Britain and the fair grounds were patronized by prince and pauper alike. With the development of the huge roundabouts, switchbacks, scenics, and all kinds of flat circular rides, the British fair grounds became a mass of humanity and spinning color. What a sight to see! As many as fifteen rides all spinning with their gaily canvassed tops, like circus wheels, organs blaring, and everyone enjoying himself immensely—for just a few pence.

In Germany, some carousels appeared in public places and amusement parks before 1850. These rides were mostly crude affairs but had some refinements, especially in the carved horses. There was no large demand for this amusement and the single efforts of wheelwrights and blacksmiths kept the fun-seeking public well supplied.

Michael Dentzel, a Kreuznach wheelwright, who in 1839 achieved some success with his carousel, was the father of Gustav A. Dentzel who was later to become the pioneer carousel builder in America. Contrary to popular belief, Michael never put his carousels on a sailboat or came to America.

There was no carousel industry in Germany and no great strides were made until the firm of Fritz Bothmann und Glück of Gotha, Thuringia, started their carousel business in 1883. Bothmann, noting the success of Savage in England and on the continent, entered the field of producing large, modern types of carousels of various designs and, within a few years, was able to compete with the English. The Bothmann construction was much simpler, less elaborate, lighter, and less expensive. Many of their two-, three-, and four-abreast makes found their way into amusement parks throughout Europe. The styles influenced some American carousel builders, however, but very, very few reached the United States, contrary to popular belief.

Bothmann also made switchbacks, airplane rides, Ferris wheels, and gondolas. Many of his horses for these machines were supplied by the Friedrich Heyn carving factory at Neustadt (Orla), started in 1870. Heyn's horses were beautifully carved but with very limited poses. They were very elegant with cut glass mirrors and etched glass ornaments decorating the carved trappings. These horses all had short backs. (Some important American auction catalogues have mistakenly listed these as "early American.")

Bothmann continued in business without Glück and in 1910 issued a ninety-six-page catalogue describing his many rides—still operated by hand or horse.

Toward the end of the nineteenth century, Joseph Hübner of Neustadt (Orla) opened his carousel works and produced a very inexpensive ride that could be hand or horse turned and was quite similar to Bothmann's hanging carousel, but instead went counterclockwise.

One Hübner, outward-facing carousel had three tiers of plush beadwork and rocking chariots. But the age of the "gas buggy" had arrived and the classical chariot was being temporarily replaced by the auto chariot. The airplane was still a novelty, and while "Josephine" was being invited for a ride on the flying machine, Hübner produced a ride which provided the thrill without the danger. This was an electrically powered airplane ride, imitated by other manufacturers.

About 1902, Hugo Haase, who was one of the leading contractors and builders of railway bridges in Germany, employed almost the entire population of Rossla in the manufacture of various amusement devices. Haase had eight carnivals on tour and kept the Rossla community busy supplying his carnivals with "Witching Waves," the "Kicking Mule," "Portable Virginia Reels," the "Figure Eight," and carousels.

Haase introduced the elaborate front or "palace enclosure" around the carousel. The most elaborate one made was brought to the United States in 1911, fronting for the "El Dorado,"

41

"Ship," "Double," "Hanging," and "Oscillating" carousels (from the catalogue of Fritz Bothmann and Glück, Gotha). The "Oscillating" carousel was turned by three or four men, made for moving carnivals, and sold for 12,000 marks.

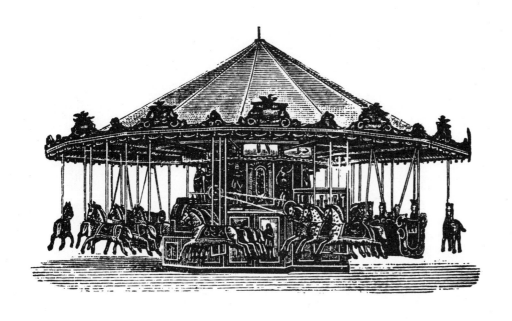

Outward-facing carousel. Built by Joseph Hübner, Neustadt, late nineteenth century.

Äroplan-Karussell (advertised by Joseph Hübner)

Der Lange Josef

Dutch *Stoomcaroussel,* entered through a ticket office with a huge carved and painted façade. This J. W. Janvier carousel shows the marvelous façade work created for these rides. (*W. J. Barlow*)

Stoomcaroussel, J. W. Janvier façade with horses and rocking gondolas on the inside. (*W. J. Barlow*)

DeEftelung, Holland, toured with this *stoomcaroussel*. (*W. J. Barlow*)

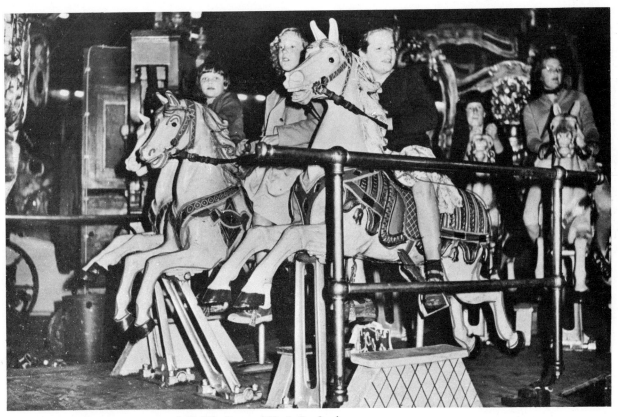

Interior of *stoomcaroussel*, DeEftelung. (*W. J. Barlow*)

Vincennes, outside Paris. (*French Government Tourist Office*)

Young lancer

Wooden horses (*French Government Tourist Office*)

French kiddie carousel

the carousel now at Steeplechase in Brooklyn. Haase was also the founder of the German fair or "Hamburg Don."

Another German manufacturer of carousels started business in 1912 and was billed as the largest carousel maker in the world—a title without challenge. His firm, known as Schippers and van der Ville, had a factory in Hamburg. Schippers, known as *Der Lange* Josef, was also His Majesty's tallest soldier. (He was captured during World War I and released after the armistice.) Unfortunately all the company's old records and photos were lost in World War II and no samples of their manufacture are available.

Quite available and in great competition throughout Europe was the "German Carousel" (now being made by Wilhelm Hennecke, of Uelzen/Hann, who started manufacture only ten years ago). Some have been imported by Morgan C. Hughes of New York and are in operation in parts of the United States.

The Dutch, like the French, Germans and other Europeans, soon adopted the carousel as their favorite entertainment.

50

CHAPTER 3

THE CAROUSEL IN AMERICA

IT HAS BEEN GENERALLY BELIEVED BY HISTORIANS THAT THE FIRST CAROUSEL IN AMERICA WAS made in 1878. However, in early America, carousels were not unknown. On August 15, 1825, while Lafayette was in Boston dedicating the monument to Bunker Hill, the Common Council of Manhattan Island, New York, granted a permit to John Sears to "establish a covered circus for a Flying Horse Establishment." But this may not have been the first carousel in America, as a petition by P. Paquet was at the same time withdrawn, indicating that his Flying Horses, perhaps exhibited earlier, may have run into trouble with the police.

Amusement parks, already a well organized, established, and profitable venture abroad, started to crop up in various regions of the young republic. They were mainly rustic resorts with crude and primitive picnic facilities for social and fraternal orders and the annual outings of the guilds. The sports were vigorous, and competitions ranged from wrestling matches, foot races, tests of strength, bowling, and shooting matches to dancing and song fests. The musicians played the numbers they had been long practicing.

In 1845, a rendezvous for the most fashionable colonials was Vauxhall Gardens, named after the contemporary English amusement park. Located in Manhattan with one entrance on Lafayette Place and another one on the Bowery, its attractions numbered a merry-go-round. Another amusement park in Manhattan, Jones Wood, a 153-acre woodland tract on the East River between Seventieth and Seventy-fifth streets, was a popular pleasure resort with several crude amusement devices, one of which was a merry-go-round. This park had excellent facilities for shooting contests, lodge outings, political rallies, and beer bouts.

Only thirty miles from New York City, along the New Jersey coast, is Long Branch. In *Frank Leslie's Weekly* of August 22, 1857, is this detailed account of the "favorite bathing resort" and its merry-go-round:

. . . beneath a large circular tent on the beach below, people are amusing themselves quite as heartily, if not in such an aristocratic manner as the waltzers and promenaders at the brilliant hotels above. Eight rotary cars were in operation and a large country wagon close by, filled with rustic Paganinis

Carousel at Long Branch, New Jersey, 1858.

and unstudied artistes, whose tremendous zeal and energy supplied all the lacking style and polish, served as a musical department. There was a great deal of fun under the same tent. In one of the cars was seated an ebon-faced daughter of Africa, gorgeous in a buff calico and pink bonnet, with a beau who officiated as a waiter during the day, turned Romeo at night. In another reclined a pretty little "star" in full ball costume, and only a lace handkerchief thrown over her plump shoulders by the side of a slender-waisted mustachiod young gallant, who had coaxed her away from the assembly room for a minute. Another was full of children, another of gray-headed people who had not yet forgotten youth and all were embodiments of solid comfort.

This merry-go-round with suspended cars was turned by a horse. The rustic band eventually gave way to the orchestrion and band organ.

Carousels were becoming popular and efforts to improve them were registered with the Patent Office. In 1850, Eliphalet S. Scripture of Green Point, New York (Brooklyn), was granted the first American carousel patent—number 7419—for the "Improvement in the Flying Horse." His invention of the galloping motion and the overhead suspension system was the first of many to follow in later years. Crude "flying horses" and other primitive types of carousels were made by wheelwrights and even farmers in the less-productive months, but there was no factory geared to manufacture them.

THE DENTZEL CAROUSEL IN AMERICA

In 1860, at the age of twenty, Gustav A. Dentzel arrived alone from Kreuznach, Germany, and opened a cabinet-making shop at 433 Brown Street in Philadelphia. Dentzel's family in Germany had experience in carousel building. An old daguerreotype, reported to date from 1839, showed the Dentzel family standing beside one of their own manufacture.

Gustav Dentzel constructed a small carousel to test the American public's reaction, found it enthusiastic, and repainted his cabinet-maker's sign to read, "G. A. Dentzel, Steam and Horsepower Caroussell Builder—1867." This was the beginning of America's pioneer carousel maker. Dentzel moved to Beach and Fairmont Avenues in Germantown, Philadelphia, and worked on making an improved carousel.

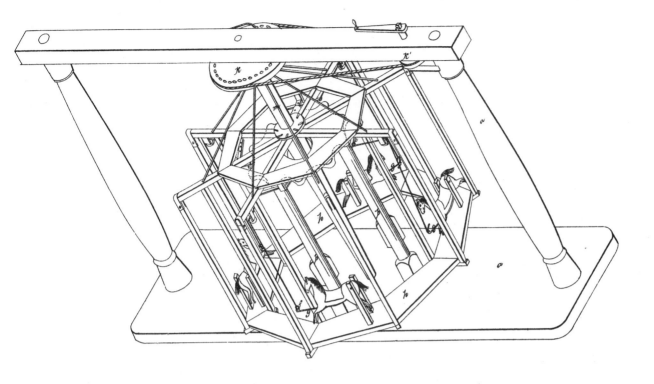

From the first American carousel patent, 1850.

Dentzel family, 1839.

At first, Dentzel worked alone, producing a small centerpole carousel with sweeps from which hung chains. Small park-type benches hung from the chains and the riders were pulled around by Dentzel himself. Daniel Muller, a Dentzel carver many years later, has related (in a letter to the author) the ride's development:

At that time, the carousel had no horses . . . just seats like park benches . . . and somebody turned the ride by hand. When I worked in the shop, there was an old book in which there were prints for all types of animals. My father said he traced the horses from that book, took it to be enlarged to working size, cut a pattern and from the pattern cut the block of wood. Then it was carved to shape.

Dentzel, in 1870, erected his first carousel at Smith's Island, a popular amusement resort with a reputation for "anything goes." It was located in the Delaware River opposite Market Street, Philadelphia. The ride became a huge success, inspiring Dentzel to dismantle it and set it up at Atlantic City, the first carousel ever at this resort.

Dentzel's first carousel, 1870.

Dentzel took the carousel on tour, stopping at Richmond, Virginia, and set it up for business. The boys, instead of wanting to ride, threw stones at Dentzel and the carousel. Dentzel protested to the police standing idly by. "Mister" they informed him, "if you want business, don't ever play 'Marching Through Georgia' in the South." Dentzel learned his lesson well and never made controversial music for his band organs.

Dentzel built other carousels, one of which he sent to Cabin John's Bridge on the Potomac River, near Washington, D. C. This also met with success, encouraging him to step up his production. In 1876, Dentzel had another carousel erected at Atlantic City. In the *National Association of Amusement Parks*, 1938, Lamarcus A. Thompson of scenic railway fame describes a visit to Dentzel.

Down by the sands at Atlantic City, I found a baby in a soap box. The box was strapped on the side of a horse next to the center pole of a Merry-Go-Round. The horse was pulling the Merry-Go-Round. In the box was little Billy Dentzel. Bill's mother was selling tickets, his father was taking up the tickets, watering the horse and looking after the Merry-Go-Round. Not only the device but the real estate on which he was riding around in the soap box was purchased by his parents at $19,000 and cost them a great struggle in making the payments as they fell due. [This same real estate in 1920 was sold by William Dentzel for $350,000.]

In Prospect Park, Brooklyn, a carousel was later established. In 1878, a familiar, although curious invitation went: "Let's go to Prospect Park Lake and take a sail on the merry-go-

54

Yacht carousel in Prospect Park, Brooklyn, 1878

round." *Harper's Weekly* had an artist sketch this ride. It shows a large circular group of boats with nine masts to which were rigged booms high enough to avoid skull crashing at the change of wind. It was propelled by wind, when available, and oarsmen when calm. This short-lived amusement had a capacity of two hundred passengers.

The close of the first century of American independence naturally called for some extraordinary and imposing commemoration of the great event. Philadelphia was gripped with excitement in anticipation of the Centennial. Great care was taken to provide the visitor with the newest and the unique in science, art, invention, and amusement. One of the attractions off the grounds was a carousel. Frank Leslie sent his reporters and illustrators to cover the Centennial and produced a twenty-five-cent comic issue *Centennial Fun*. The Centennials' "Patent Cosmopolitan Carousal" came in for its share of caricature. This carousel may have been made by Dentzel or C. W. F. Dare of Greenpoint, Brooklyn, who was also making amusement devices at this time.

Carousel in Central Park, New York City, 1872.

Carousel at the Philadelphia Centennial, 1876.

Gustav A. Dentzel

In 1885 Dentzel produced this machine and others similar to it (shown in his first catalogue). Lions, a giraffe, and swan chariots joined the camels and horses used in earlier carousels. The menagerie was soon to grow as was the size of his rides.

Dentzel had already applied steam as the motive power; its first use was at a site known as "Excursion House." The size and quality of his carousels improved and demands for his creations came from various parts of the country. Dentzel prospered and moved his shop to larger quarters adjoining his home at 3635–41 Germantown Avenue in Germantown, Philadelphia. Dentzel now required three floors to handle the orders that were coming in, and to supply himself with the rides he now operated in various public parks and amusement centers. His income from these operations exceeded by far his proceeds from manufacture.

In 1890, Dentzel, who was always experimenting with new ideas to attract new business at Atlantic City, erected a "Two-story" carousel. While it created amazement, it was too cumbersome, making the loading and unloading of passengers too slow to be profitable. It was dismantled, Dentzel using parts for other carousels.

Dentzel's carousels were now large three- and four-abreast rides costing $20,000. They were lavishly decorated, finely carved, and sold to many seaside resorts, amusement parks, and countries abroad. Dentzel successfully operated carousels at Atlantic City, Willow Grove, New Jersey, and many other places.

Dentzel's friend, Muller, died and left two young boys, Albert and Daniel in his care. Dentzel raised and educated the Muller boys, giving them employment in his shop. Both boys developed into excellent carvers, especially Daniel, who also had artistic talent. Upon maturity, the Mullers left Dentzel, competing with him in the manufacture of carousels. They specialized in making very fine horse-drawn carousel chariots. Their business was not successful and Dentzel, who never forgave them, refused to re-employ them.

By 1903, Dentzel's factory was a busy crowded affair with orders piled up, waiting to be assembled and sent out. On the first floor of the Dentzel factory were the tooling and carving machinery in charge of Harry Ernest Dentzel, a nephew. The second floor was the carving room; the third floor contained the paint shop. Out in the yard was a large shed used in constructing the frames, platforms, and rims, each in separate sections. Henry Paul supervised this operation, never working from a plan or blueprint. All the measurements were committed to memory, but with micrometer accuracy, Paul never erred. In the spring of each year an old man who was a schooner-mast maker came to work in the yard, made five or more center-poles, and disappeared until the following spring.

Dentzel had to enlarge the factory and built on the property next to his home. About this time, Dentzel's son, William, built a very showy carousel which became Dentzel's favorite. This carousel, upon which he had lavished time, money, and effort, appeared in Woodside Park, Philadelphia. It became a sensation. Dentzel often drove his customers to the park, showed this sample and usually pocketed an order. This carousel, now owned by the author is operating in the Music Circus at Lambertville, New Jersey.

Gustav A. Dentzel died on January 22, 1909. The plant shut down until the estate was cleared and reopened under the direction of his son, William H. Dentzel. Bill or "Hobby-Horse Bill" as he was affectionately called by his friends, made an even greater success of the business, constructing large showy carousels of his own design. Bill worked in the carving shop for many years and was familiar with all phases of production. (One such carousel, operated for Dentzel by the comedian Billy Ritchie, was at Rockaway Beach on Long Island.) Bill Dentzel had many friends, was very well liked, and had many business associations, including one with Louis Berni in the making of carousel organs. William H. Dentzel died in 1928. The depression had arrived, and there was no demand for carousels. His great establishment came to an end under the auctioneer's hammer on January 18, 1929.

The National Association of Amusement Parks praised the younger Dentzel by voting the following resolution:

He kept raising the ideals higher and higher, building a finer and more artistic, more serviceable product than either of his sires, and had he lived to 1937, the merry-go-round would have been built in one family continuously and uninterruptedly for one complete century. The knights of old rode their magnificently caparisoned horses only in defense of themselves and their honor and to what they thought is their lasting way of fame. Our member produced a finer caparisoned horse than the world had known up to his time, and best of all, it was produced to give joy to the millions, and any man who had made his fellow man happy, cannot be said to have lived his life in vain.

Dentzel's favorite carousel

William H. Dentzel

Dentzel, "Two-story" carousel, 1890. The ring basket (*center left*) was standard equipment, but the palm-fan air-conditioning reveals the Dentzel touch.

Carousel at Rockaway Beach, Long Island.

Carousel, Coney Island, 1876. The builder, Charles I. D. Looff, stands between the drummer and clarinettist in the tall hat. (*Arthur R. Simmons*)

THE LOOFF CAROUSEL

Coney Island, the world-famous seaside resort in Brooklyn has had many famous carousels. None was more historic than the first carousel in 1876 made by Charles I. D. Looff of Brooklyn. This carousel was placed on the grounds of Balmer's Pavilion on West Sixth Street and Surf Avenue. In 1878, it was sold to a Street Railroad company, but Looff, sentimentally, bought it back forty-two years later.

Born on May 2, 1852 in Schleswig-Holstein, Charles I. D. Looff came to New York on August 14, 1870, and listed himself as a carver at 526 Leonard Street in Greenpoint, Brooklyn. He worked as a woodcarver in a furniture factory, but during his spare time at home, usually early dawn, carved wooden animals. He painted and assembled them on the frame and platform he had erected at Coney Island. This merry-go-round became an instant success encouraging Looff to make more.

Opening a factory at Bedford Avenue and Guernsey Street, Brooklyn, Looff, in 1880, placed another carousel in the beer garden at Feltman's facing Surf Avenue at Coney Island. He then made a third carousel and placed it at Young's Pier in Atlantic City. The throngs flocked to this ride. Young made a handsome offer to purchase it from Looff, who accepted it, launching himself well into the merry-go-round business. Looff did much of the carving himself, his horses and figures being highly prized by collectors today. Like Dentzel, he made a "Two-story" carousel which he discarded for the same reasons. In 1892, Looff built a Ferris wheel at Rocky Point, Rhode Island, having become attracted to this area.

62

By 1895, Looff was building huge carousels. His carousel at Crescent Park, Riverside, Rhode Island (now operated by his grandson, Arthur R. Simmons) has sixty-two horses and four chariots.

In 1905, the City of New York, in planning a park, condemned the property upon which the Looff factory stood. Looff, having previously built another factory at Riverside, moved with his family in 1905–6. Looff's shop foreman, Timothy Murphy, was put in charge of operating the Looff carousel at Crescent Park, Rhode Island, and given a quarter interest. Looff had an argument with Murphy, fired him, and Murphy sued for his quarter interest. Murphy won. While judgment was pending, Looff erected a carousel in a tent opposite Crescent Park, along the waterfront. Later, he partially dismantled it, floating the carousel to Narragansett Pier. Looff built a domed building at the pier, but it had no success and was removed.

Charles I. D. Looff (*Arthur R. Simmons*)

CH. LOOFF
Riverside. R.I.

Various styles of Looff carousels and animals. In 1909, Looff himself carved a very fine carousel with fifty-four animals, presenting it to his daughter Emma Looff Vogel as a wedding present.

Another of Looff's great carousels is at Goddard State Park, Rhode Island, owned by Joseph Carrolo, now eighty-seven, the oldest carousel operator in the country. Carrolo worked for Looff for many years, starting as a ring boy.

In August of 1910, Looff moved his factory to Ocean Park, California, shortly thereafter, deciding on Long Beach as a permanent home. Looff put through a deal involving $150,000 whereby he came into possession of property on the pike, buying up leases to install the hippodrome.

Looff built an apartment for himself and his family on the second story. Later, he erected a large factory on West Sixth Street, in the local harbor district, for the manufacture of amusement equipment. Looff also made many portable carousels, but he specialized in the large machines. Almost all of the large ones were pit carousels. To give a jumping motion to his horses without infringement on existing patents, he designed his rides so that the horse rods could go below the level of the platform on its downward stroke. As much as a three foot pit was needed. This made the pit carousel impractical for out-of-doors. Looff died on July 1, 1918, at Long Beach, California, leaving behind rings of gentle ponies.

Looff's brother-in-law, Fred Dolle, operated a carousel at Coney Island Brooklyn, from 1907 to 1913. During the winter months he made two or three carousels. Charles Carmel carved the horses, Dolle building the structures with the help of M. D. Borelli. (Carousels do get around. Dolle made a carousel to be operated for himself at Fairy Land Park, then in Westchester, New York. The park closed, sending the carousel to its new owners, the Ragamosa Brothers at Savin Rock, Connecticut. The carousel operated there for a number of years but turned up at Wildwood, New Jersey, where it is still in operation.) Dolle died in 1913, his widow, with the help of Borelli, kept the plant in operation for a few more years.

BIGGER AND BETTER CAROUSELS

The famous merry-go-round at Watch Hill, Rhode Island was made about 1876 and is accredited to a Babcock of Troy, New York. The horses bear a familiar resemblance to the Dentzel machine at Kreuznach, Germany. This is a flying horse type carousel; the swifter it went—the more tilted the rider. Chains control the arc and provide safety. This is the oldest-known still-active carousel operating in the United States. First hand driven, then horse powered, water powered, and now electrified.

New ideas were welcome in the improvement of the carousel. The amusement parks and seashore resorts were looking for new forms of entertainment and novelty rides to attract the patrons. Partly for this reason, William Sassack of Brooklyn patented a roundabout on June 12, 1888, combining the thrills of a balloon ascension with the carousel. (A variation of this was produced thirty years later.) Schofield's "Traveling Carousel," never manufactured, combined the scenic railway idea with the merry-go-round. The "engineer" sat in the center guiding the ride. No cowcatchers were attached.

Many of these patented and some borrowed ideas found their way into amusement parks. The parks in many cases were built and operated by the street railway companies who extended trolly lines to the outskirts of towns, creating these picnic and amusement areas to attract added fares. One such trolly park is Kennywood, on the banks of the historic Monongahela River, eleven miles from Pittsburgh. The park, originally a picnic grove, was owned by Thomas J. Kenny who bought it in 1818 for a few pounds and threw in a barrel of whiskey to seal the deal. Kenny became rich when coal was later discovered on his 365 acres. The Mellon family of Pittsburgh leased 141 acres in 1898 from Kenny and built a trolly park. A carousel was one of the many attractions.

Flying horses, Watch Hill. (*Lily Carlson*)

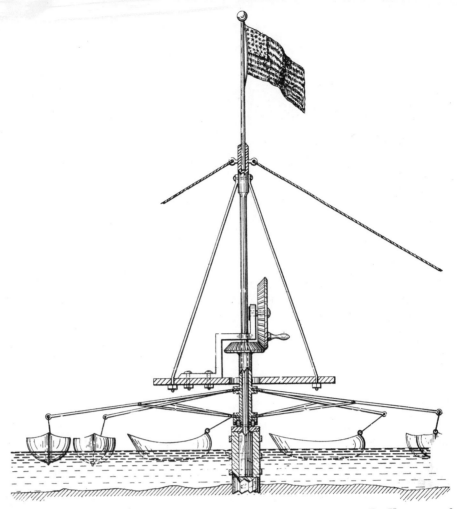

"Marine and Land" merry-go-round, 1888. Patented by John R. Kennett of Syracuse, New York. This was the forerunner of the present-day kiddie boat ride. (*U.S. Patent Office Records*)

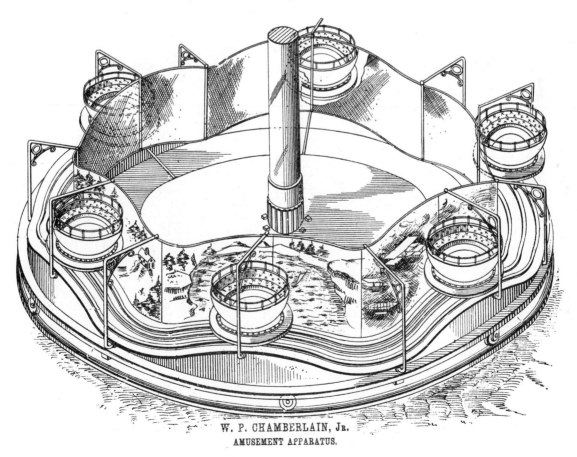

W. P. CHAMBERLAIN, Jr.
AMUSEMENT APPARATUS.

"Lovers' Tubs," 1910. Patented by W. P. Chamberlain, Jr. The action was designed to throw couples into each others arms, creating the excuse for a public embrace. (*U.S. Patent Office Records*)

A sketch of the State Fair Grounds near Richmond, Virginia, by Joseph Baker visiting from England, 1883. Following the Civil War, Negroes, who had obtained citizenship status by the enactment of the 14th Amendment in 1868, were nevertheless excluded from most public facilities. Among these were carousels and places of amusement. Their exclusion had become a national controversy and was ended by Congress with the enactment of the Civil Rights Act of 1875. But the law was declared unconstitutional by the Supreme Court in 1883 on the ground that such rights could be protected only by the state governments. This led to the adoption of civil rights laws by some Northern states, but the Southern states took no action.

"Balloon" carousel, 1888. (*U.S. Patent Office Records*)

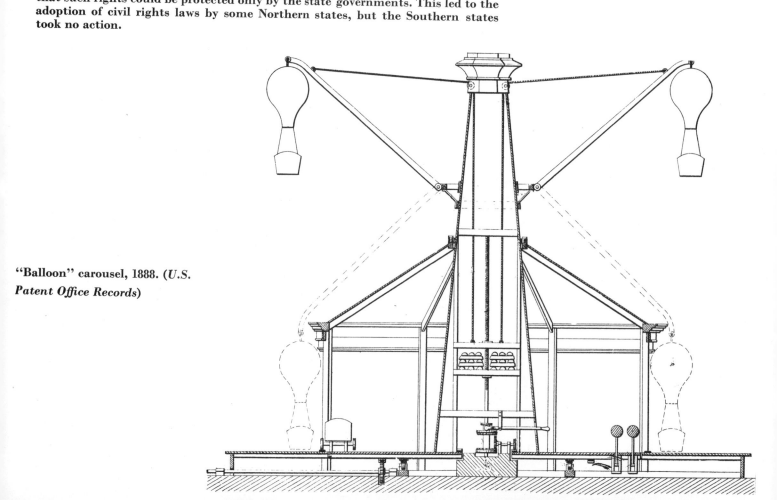

Ulmer Park, Gravesend, Brooklyn, is typical of the trolly park. The trolly brought the passengers to the entrance, taking home full cars of early picnickers.

Allan Herschell, originator of the Tonawanda merry-go-round.

THE HERSCHELL CAROUSEL

The best known carousel maker—still making carousels—is the Allan Herschell Company Inc. at Buffalo, New York, originally located in neighboring North Tonawanda. At one time the name "North Tonawanda" was magic throughout the land. It was the home of three carousel factories and the birthplace of the American band organ, and one of the important names in northern New York was Allan Herschell.

Allan Herschell was born in Arbreath, Forfarshire, Scotland, on April 27, 1851. He learned the trade of molder in his youth and on August 14, 1870, came to America with his parents. His first job was with the Buffalo Scale Company in 1870. The next year, he went to Canada, returned, and took a job in 1872 as foreman in the Dr. Kreball and Company trip hammer factory. It failed, Herschell tried his luck in Boston but returned when his mother took ill. That year, he met James Armitage, and together, they opened a factory on Main Street, Williamsville, New York.

In the fall of 1872, George Zent induced Armitage and Herschell to come to Tonawanda, and with Alexander Kent, they built a factory at Sweeney Street near the docks. The firm, known as the Tonawanda Engine and Machine Company, opened for business on election day, 1873. In 1874, Allan's brother George joined the firm. Misfortune soon set in: the shop burned down in 1876, was rebuilt, and burned again the same year. Herschell, together

70

with Armitage, built a new factory at Oliver and Mechanic Streets in 1876. The new Armitage Herschell Company made machinery and boilers. Armitage was president, Herschell was vice-president, and his brother George became treasurer. In 1882, Allan Herschell married Ida Spillman and a long business relationship later developed with her brothers. In 1890 the firm was reorganized under the name, Armitage Herschell Company and incorporated for $150,000. Over a hundred workmen were employed in the manufacture of steam engines and boilers, also, mill and agricultural machinery. A steam riding gallery was listed as one of their products.

Armitage Herschell steam riding gallery, first built in 1883.

The decision in 1882 to build a steam riding gallery resulted from Herschell's visit to New York City seeking medical aid for an attack of ague. Herschell related that while stopping at Hornell, New York, he decided on the carousel. Returning home, he built his first steam riding gallery in 1883, against the strong opposition of his partners. He gave it trials in Tonawanda, Niagara Falls, Williamsville, Lancaster, Cowlesville, and Attica. At Attica, he sold it to Mr. Coons, an auctioneer. Returning home, he built another, his second in 1884, selling it to Sam Dietrick of Niagara Falls. He completed his third machine in 1885 and ran it in Buffalo. A half-interest in the ride was sold to Christ Krull of Martinsville, both he and Herschell taking it to New Orleans for a twelve-week run. Proving a success, in spite of its many breakdowns, the machine was sold to Krull by Allan Herschell. After writing his partners of his troubles, a reply came, reading, "Throw same in canal and return to North Tonawanda, plenty of work at foundry." Herschell was furious and sent no mail for two months.

Bert Stickney, who in 1885 helped lay out, build, and run the third machine at the World Exposition and Cotton Centennial in New Orleans, recalled that event in a 1924 Spillman Engineering Corp. house publication.

It took a cowboy to ride it and it beats all that people were so crazy to ride that we had a devil of time to keep them from overloading the machine which had 24 prancing horses and four chariots. This machine was of the track type with hinged horses driven by eccentrics. Electric lights were undreamed of so we lighted the machine with gasoline torches which smoked, filling the canvas top with gasoline fumes. Then too, there was the steam engine and the boiler that burned soft coal generating about as much smoke as it did steam. When the wind blew the smoke toward the machine, some of the people who had paid a perfectly good nickel to ride, were a sweet looking sight. Believe me, the public wouldn't stand for that now-a-days. Everything's got to be ginger bread or you don't get their money.

71

Second Annual Outing, July 3rd, 1902. Most of these Spillman-Herschell employees were with the original Armitage Herschell Company and some of these built the first carousel for the firm. Allan Herschell stands second from left in the third row. *(Roy L. Herschell)*

In 1887, a more complete and perfected gallery was offered for sale, became popular, and in 1890, sixty machines were sold: the following year, one hundred steam riding galleries were sold. By 1891, one machine a day was being shipped to many parts of the country. Herschell went abroad, making a stop in Bombay, India, in 1894 and stayed to operate the ride for six months, sending back orders for steam riding galleries, one for a maharajah and his entourage and another for a sultan to amuse his harem. The company's books now were showing a gain of $200,000.

Competition began in neighboring Lockport. Two firms started manufacture of almost the identical machine. Hundreds of these machines were made and operated with great financial success. Today, only four are known to exist; among these, one is in storage at the Henry Ford Museum in Dearborn, Michigan, and Gaslight Village at Lake George, New York, has one in operating order.

THE HERSCHELL-SPILLMAN COMPANY AND COMPETITORS

So much money was made by the Armitage Herschell firm that it was said, the banks would not take their deposits. Armitage Herschell invested heavily in real estate. The 1899 land-boom bubble burst, forcing the company into receivership. A struggle for control took place.

72

Herschell, with his brother-in-law, Edward Spillman, formed a new company, opening a new factory at 162–198 Sweeney Street. In 1903, they bought out the failing Armitage Herschell Company, and with the two facilities became the largest manufacturer of carousels in the country, calling themselves the Herschell-Spillman Company.

Steam boiler

A 1913 Herschell-Spillman catalogue shows various models of the same Tonawanda machine with the cone-shaped wheels put back toward the center. The steam boiler was still the motive power and the rides were primitive compared to the huge showy carousels of most of their competitors. However, it was still possible to buy a carousel for less than $2000 from the Herschell-Spillman Company.

By 1913, the Herschell-Spillman two-abreast was the most advanced model made. It was to be had with steam power, gasoline engine, or electric motor. Rocker forks below the horses were a new invention used to give the horses a galloping motion as they were suspended from overhead. This method was not as practical as others in use but was one, which would not infringe on existing patents. Allan Herschell had been bothered for some years by sieges of ague. At Tonawanda, which the Indians named "the Swamp," the dampness worsened his condition and Herschell was forced to retire, selling his interests in the company in 1911.

73

Steam riding gallery No. 1 (Herschell-Spillman catalogue, 1913). Shown without the tent. It was powered by a double cylinder back-geared steam engine. It had twenty-four horses, four chariots, and was forty feet in diameter.

"Twoabreast" (Herschell-Spillman catalogue, 1913).

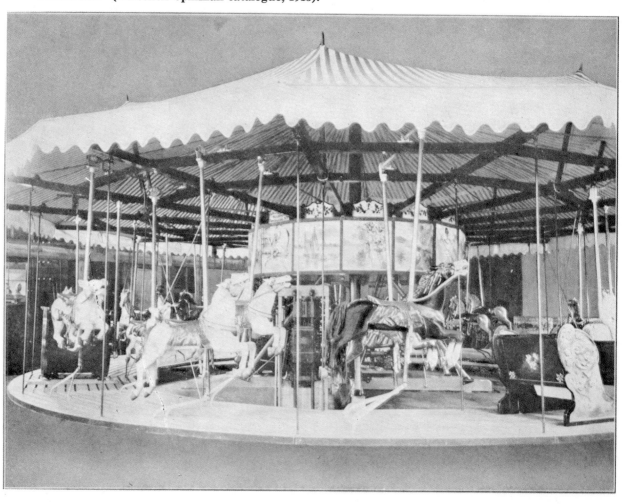

Hand-powered gallery (Herschell-Spillman catalogue, 1913). It had twelve horses, two chariots, and was twenty-four feet in diameter.

But he returned in 1915. John Wendler and Fred Fritchie formed the Allan Herschell Company with Herschell as president. In 1920, what remained of the Herschell-Spillman Company was reorganized and the following notice was released by the new Spillman Engineering Corporation:

The Herschell-Spillman Motor Company have recently undergone some changes in their reorganization whereby the amusement riding department was taken over by men who have long been in charge of this department. The Herschell-Spillman Motor Company, building four cylinder engines, have grown extensively in the past few years and several large additions to the factory have been necessary. Now, another large addition will be built and this structure will occupy the space formerly used by the amusement department of the business. Men interested in the amusement riding device part of the business have purchased all the building formerly used for that purpose and will dismantle them, building a new modern factory on the site once used by the Armitage Herschell Company. Officers of the firm which is incorporated under the name of Spillman Engineering Corporation, are: E. O. Spillman, president; George H. Cramer, vice president & general manager; A. M. Hathaway, secretary and Albert Spillman, treasurer.

In addition to these men the same carving foreman, carpenter foreman, foreman of the decorating departments and foreman of the general construction formerly with the Herschell-Spillman Company will be identified with the new Spillman Company.

The know-how of the Spillman group produced a line of notable machines. Spillman made many park carousels of three- and four-abreast—fifty feet in diameter size. They also produced two- and three-abreast portables, the Spillman, Jr., thirty-two feet in diameter, and wagons. Their 1923 catalogue also listed carousels with large size figures—a lion, tiger, ostrich, stork, giraffe, charging horse, armored horse, deer, goat, zebra, rooster, frog, dog, cat, trotting, and galloping horses.

In 1923, Allan Herschell retired from the presidency of the Allan Herschell Company and was succeeded by former senator James P. MacKensie. Herschell died in 1927 and in 1945 the Allan Herschell Company bought out the Spillman Engineering Corporation. The new president, John Wendler, was once a carousel-horse painter in the Armitage-Herschell Company.

Spillman Engineering Corporation officers. Left, Al. Spillman, center, George Cramer, right, M. A. Spillman.

George H. Cramer of the Spillman Engineering Corporation (in the white cap) shown with his first carousel at Marshall, Indiana, July 3rd, 1902.

Spillman fifty-foot park carousel

The impression had been created (and persists) that the first carousel in America was built by Carl Landow and his cousin, Carl Newman, at Wolcottsburg, New York, in 1878. Such belief could result only from ignorance of the accomplishments of earlier American carousel makers.

Sometime about 1879, Carl Landow, a German cabinet maker by trade, arrived in America and settled in Wolcottsburg, now Clarence Center, New York. His brother-in-law, Carl Newman, had arrived a few years earlier with his family and settled on a farm at Goodrich and Brauer Roads. Landow had ideas about making a carousel patterned after some he had seen in rural Germany. Newman was not enthusiastic as the community was composed of God-fearing Germans who frowned upon amusements and their devilish devices.

Newman finally acceded and Landow carved crude horses from local basswood, painted them and gave them real hair tails. Newman made the platform, and the working parts. The carousel was set up on the grounds of a tavern and the public was invited to ride for a nickel. The carousel was enthusiastically received and taken on tour throughout the countryside. It was later sold to a Mr. Gumbert from North Clarence. Later, he added steam power to the ride and also traveled about with it. (One of the horses from this carousel was once part of the Mangel's Museum of Public Recreation in Coney Island and is now at the Circus Hall of Fame in Sarasota, Florida). This lone primitive effort of Landow and Newman gave great pleasure to many but contributed little to the development of the carousel.

Landow-Newman carousel, 1879.

As noted earlier, with the success of the Armitage Herschell steam-powered Tonawanda carousel, competition arose in nearby Lockport, New York. The firm of Norman and Evans whose plant was "in the hollow near the state yards at the foot of the Erie Canal lock" manufactured dredges, steam shovels, steam derricks, steam canal-boat machinery, etc. The great carousel-building activity in the neighboring "Lumber City" of Tonawanda was eyed with envy, and Norman and Evans, who had ample facilities, produced their first carousel. Joshua Wilber, unofficial historian of Lockport, jotted down the event in a shorthand of his own design, his story appearing in the *Lockport Daily Journal* on July 11, 1891. Under the heading, "The New Merry-Go-Round" the story followed:

The first steam riding-gallery ever built in this city was exhibited Thursday evening on the grounds of the Pound Manufacturing Co. near the foot of the Locks. The employees and their wives were invited by the builder, Norman & Evans to go down and try the machine free of charge which they did to the delight of all. Only invited guests were expected to ride but as is usually the case, a number of outsiders were there and enjoyed the exhilaratory sport with the rest of them . . . loaded to the fullest capacity, the machine rotated with that even motion of the stationary sets and the rocking movement of the horses, which were so much desired.

Conspicuous among its many interesting features is the fine workmanship. The horses were built of 2 inch plank and are exceedingly light and ornamental. A neat canvas tent encloses the affair, while outside a small upright engine rapidly turns the endless cable which revolves the gallery. It is a nice outfit to be sure, but it comes high—something like $2,600, the average price on the market. The machine yesterday was taken down, carefully packed and shipped to Kansas.

A colorful booklet issued by Norman and Evans described the machine in detail. It was almost identical to the Armitage Herschell steam riding gallery even to "a magnificent organ, in a highly finished case, accompan[ying] each machine. The organ is operated by power from the engine, but it is ingeniously contrived so that it appears to be driven by the figure of a Negro boy whose hand is on the crank."

William L. Norman and Spalding Evans, both native born, continued making these machines, introducing in 1898 the first steam switchback merry-go-round to America. It had an undulating motion, operating eight cars designed to represent Venetian gondolas. Each car carried twelve passengers. The ride had a capacity of ninety-six passengers and like its English prototype went clockwise. It had a center engine which belched black soft-coal smoke from its centerpole smokestack. It had a band organ designed by Eugene DeKleist of nearby

William L. Norman (*left*) and Spalding Evans (*right*).

78

Steam merry-go-round, Norman and Evans, 1890's.

Tonawanda. The engine was designed and built by Wallace Butterick and George Bounsall. The woodwork done by Norman E. Arnold and the scroll lettering and painting by Andrew Savigney. The decorative carved work was profuse—its designer, Charles Emmet of Boston. The idea was suggested to Norman and Evans by William R. Insham, a native of Birmingham, England, who had been in this country only two years. The switchback, a great novelty here, was sold to George P. Koetz who placed it in Shenley Park, Pittsburgh. Its later history is unknown.

This success spurred the formation of a new organization called The American Merry-Go-Round and Novelty Company. It was incorporated on November 9, 1898 with headquarters in Lockport. This company made a switchback with ten gondolas; unlike the Norman and Evans product, it was driven by electricity, with a claim that it was the first electrically-driven merry-go-round ever manufactured. It had a ten horsepower Keystone motor and a two horsepower motor for the band organ made by the North Tonawanda Band Organ Company. The same workmen who had designed and produced the Norman and Evans switchback also made this. It was sold to T. J. Ninns of Cleveland and was to be located in the Sans Souci Park in Chicago. But the firm had very little capital and was dissolved in 1901.

Norman and Evans made about seventy-five machines each year until the death of William L. Norman on November 13, 1904. Spalding Evans continued the business under the name Evans and Company until 1905. He died on March 13, 1923.

Another company, Owen and Margeson made steam-operated carousels at Hornellsville (now Hornell), New York from 1893 to 1896. Their operation was small with very few machines reaching the public. Advertisements appeared in weeklies read largely by farmers and rural folk.

America rode happily along to the chugging of the steam engines and the blare of the band organ, each keeping its own tempo, delighting young and old alike.

In the mid-nineties, Gottfried Bungarz's Stage, Wagon and Carrousele Works was established in Brooklyn making merry-go-rounds on order. The extant engraving of an umbrella-covered menagerie graphically details his manufacture. Although an important name, very little is known about Bungarz. His business solicitations claim "experience in this line of work,

Bungarz carousel, 1890's.

extending over thirty years." However, there exists a bill of sale of a Bungarz carousel for $1140 with interest thereon at the rate of six percent per annum, showing that George W. Kremer of North Beach, Long Island, now the site of LaGuardia Airport, was the purchaser. Bungarz was said to have built a carousel in 1886, which was located at the entrance to the old Sea Beach Palace on Surf Avenue in Coney Island, and others at Spuyten Duyvel, New York; South Beach, Long Island; Asbury Park, New Jersey, and one on Fifteenth Street and Fifth Avenue, Brooklyn.

Bungarz nameplate which was fastened to the backs of seats or chariots

In Central Park, New York, the old merry-go-round was replaced with a more modern ride. It was driven by a mule hitched to the centerpole which extended below the platform into the basement. Stopping and starting signals were given by taps on the wooden floor. Mr. Isaacs, the manager, would often run outside and chase the children lying on their stomachs peeking into the basement windows, watching the mule. In 1912, an electric motor replaced the mule. In 1954, a fire partially destroyed the ride. It was bought by a Bronx beach club, refurbished, run for several years, and sold. Its present location is unknown.

In Tonawanda, in 1893, Gillie, Godard and Company made steam riding galleries and "Whirling Panoramas." The use of the word "gallery" was contested by Herschell and it was dropped. George A. Gillie at one time was part of the original Tonawanda Engine & Machine Company. The "Whirling Panorama" consisted of a painted canvas hung from the top of the tent around the center or outside. The scenes painted on order ranged from buffalo hunts to tropical lagoons, to inspire the riders on their imaginative trips. Little more was made; Gillie without Godard manufactured panoramas until 1900.

A tremendous stimulus was given to the carousel industry in America in 1894 by Frank C. Bostock when he imported and erected in Coney Island an English roundabout. It had galloping horses actuated by an overhead cranking system invented by Frederick Savage of Kings Lynn, England. Previously, many carousels with rocking horses, especially the Tonawanda type, had been built, but these depended on the track on which the structure revolved, the cone-shaped wheels, and the hinged horses.

The English system had the entire structure suspended from a central mast. This system had been used in America for many years but had not included the galloping horse mechanism. The new method eliminated the track, giving the wooden horses a smooth floating, galloping motion. This was soon accepted, improved upon and is in use today.

Almost within a brass ring's throw of the Charles I. D. Looff factory in Greenpoint, Brooklyn, was the carousel factory of Charles W. F. Dare, called the N. Y. Carousal Manufacturing Company. It was located at 234 Kent Street, produced three types of carousels and a great amount of other amusement equipment, such as shooting galleries, swings, cane boards, strength testers, bowling alleys, goat phaetons, and various carousel accessories.

Dare was one of the earliest makers of amusement equipment in America. In 1870, he made a wooden Ferris wheel, then called the Dare wheel. Dare may have also made a steam riding gallery but no conclusive proof exists for this early date. The Brooklyn directory's first listing of Dare's connection with carousels appears in the 1890–91 edition. In March

Dare's "Galloping Horses" rode on a flat revolving platform and had iron wheels that ran on a circular track. It was steam powered and commonly known as the "Tonawanda" type machine.

1899, the *New York Times Illustrated Magazine* was impressed sufficiently with the manufacture and production to send a reporter to Dare's factory who reported the following (reproduced in part):

Those with horses or other figures hanging from rods are called, "Flying Horses." The "Galloping Horses," or "Steam Riding Galleries" on which wooden animals move up and down were originally introduced here from England. These, however, have been Americanized and the figures made much lighter than the imported ones. In some parts of the country, they are also called "Flying Jennys." They were so called to distinguish them from the machine with a swinging platform.

A carousel costs from $300 to $10,000 according to the decoration and finish. A wooden figure of a prancing horse with its right foreleg gracefully raised, cost from $14 to $35, according to size. Brass and looking glass ornaments are added when desired and cost more. Zebras cost the same as horses and a meek goat brings the same price as a fierce lion. A carousel that will seat 60 riders measures 40 feet in diameter and costs $2,200. This is intended to be a permanent attraction in a large amusement hall in a principal city. Eighteen arms run through the center pole sustaining 3 rows of figures and the swinging platform is wide and roomy. The figures consist of 11 horses, 14 inches in body diameter, 1 camel, 1 elephant, 1 deer, and one lion each 14 inches around and all on the outer row. Next, 11 horses, 12 inches around and a camel, elephant, deer, lion of the same dimensions. Then comes 11 horses, 10 inches around, 2 donkeys and 3 double seated dragon or shell chariots. These are finished with jewels on the figures and looking glass reflectors which are added to suit the purchaser. A machine of this size requires a powerful engine to drive the platform and organ.

In this large factory in Brooklyn, 25 carvers are kept at work all year round, carving animals for these machines. One well-known manufacturer of carousels in this city has a private one at his country seat in Connecticut upon which he frequently entertains his friends.

Billboard Magazine never carried one of their ads and except for a very early seventy-two-page catalogue, no record of their advertisements appear. The Brooklyn directory has no listing for either Dare or the firm after 1898.

82

Dare's "Hanging Figures," twenty-six feet in diameter, had ten arms from which hung sixteen horses and two swinging chariots. It seated twenty-six riders and came complete with awning, side curtains, hand-power attachment, ornamental circle, ring box, rings, spears, decorations, flags, etc. for $550.

"Swinging Platform" carousel. Built by Dare, it was operated by hand, horse, or steam. It had twenty-four animals and two, double-seat dragon or shell chariots and sold for $1,050, complete.

Up to the 1890's, all the carousel factories were in the East. Orders were coming in from all parts of the United States, and flat cars making long hauls were loaded with the new amusement rides. To fill this need closer to home, Charles Wallace Parker opened his factory at Abilene, Kansas, to manufacture shooting galleries and carousels, and of all the carousel makers, Parker had the most colorful, exciting, and varied career.

Charles Wallace Parker was born on April 26, 1864, in Griggsville, Illinois. His mother was a niece of the author of *Vanity Fair*, William Makepeace Thackeray. When Parker was five years old, his family moved by prairie schooner to Abilene, Kansas. In his youth, Parker farmed, trying to wrest a living from the unresponsive soil. Then, he received his first and only political appointment, "Knight of the Broom and Pan," using Parker's own words, or Janitor of the new Dickinson County Court House at Abilene. His salary was $32.00 a month.

Parker saved some money from his meagre salary and with a capital of $3.75 ordered a target and guns from the Schmelzer Arms Company of Leavenworth, Kansas, at a cost of $18.00. In a short time, when it was paid for, Parker then decided to build his own shooting galleries. Parker and three partners purchased a second-hand carousel. After touring the neighboring territory, the partners tired of this nomad existence, but Parker found it an exciting life. He bought out their interests in the carousel and became sole owner. He improved his shooting galleries and kept tinkering and making improvements on the carousel. Parker was convinced that he could make a better one and after 1892 produced his first new carousel.

Parker then sold his first carousel to his brother, Will T. Parker. In 1893 or 1894 he enlarged his factory on the South side of Abilene to twice its former size and increased his force to five workmen. The sign read, "Parker Carnival Supply Company."

The carnival and its excitement attracted Parker, influencing him to not only make the equipment but operate it himself. In a few years, Parker's literature had a picture of himself on the cover pointing in the direction of huge mills with smoke belching from the chimneys.

Right across the tracks from the Parker factory at Abilene, was the Eisenhower home. Stories have long persisted that our former president sanded horses in the Parker factory. In Alden Hatch's, *General Ike* (Henry Holt & Co.), the story also appears mentioning Eisenhower's sandpapering chores. The year appears to be 1906 when Ike was but fourteen or fifteen years old.

Charles Wallace Parker, the "amusement king."

One of Parker's shows being loaded. A carousel can be seen in the center. Parker coined the name "carry-us-all" for his carousels, stating that he heard some Negro riders calling it that. It became a Parker identification. (*Seth Barter, Jr.*)

Early Parker carousel, photographed at Gainsville, Texas, 1909. The chariot, quite primitive, does not seem to fit with the exquisite horse behind it. (*Seth Barter, Jr.*)

Live horses pulling a wooden-horse carry-us-all

Parker, by 1911, was making jumping horse carousels, Ferris wheels, carved wagon-fronts and monkey speedways, using live monkeys as auto drivers in a fixed course. He also equipped complete carnival companies, mechanical shooting galleries, portable electric-lighting plants, Pullman, baggage, and flat cars, illusions, concessions, handpainted banners and show fronts, and tent tops with side walls. Parker also claimed to be manufacturing band organs and orchestrions. The Abilene factory was too small to contain all the facilities for his new enterprises. Parker announced on February 1, 1911, the opening of his new factory and removal to Leavenworth, Kansas.

Carry-us-alls on the roof of the Parker factory

In April, 1917, there were in production at the Parker factory, seventeen carry-us-alls, five Ferris wheels and three monkey speedways. All were set up and being tested simultaneously. Even the roof and front yard were pressed into service and at one time there were seven carry-us-alls on the roof.

Parker employed a very capable public relations man whose title was Manager of Sales and Publicity. G. H. Fishbach glorified the exploits of his boss and endowed him with an aura of saintliness. One sixty-four-page Parker publication was almost completely devoted to proving the clean character and moral superiority of the Parker shows. The following is from the Argenta, Arkansas, *Daily News*, 1907:

C. W. Parker is a man who, by untiring efforts, has rescued the carnival business from the gutter, where it had sunk when the hoochy-koochy and snake eating rage hit the country. There are none of these disgusting freaks and maids, whose twistings have made the streets of Cairo the tropical center of the universe, to be found around the Parker shows. Of course, the so-called game sport—but more correctly speaking, the tin horn variety—when he finds that little Egypt is not on the staff immediately informs his pals that the Parker Pike is a dead one.

The *Bedouin*, Parker's house organ, edited by Fishbach, was almost completely devoted to the glorification of Parker, his products, and his family, whose pictures graced the covers.

Parker's carousels, made mainly for transport, were light. Parker made two-, three-, and four-abreast jumping horse carry-us-alls. However, he made three fifty-foot platform carousels all in the same year. One of these, still active, is owned by W. J. Betts of Redondo, Washington.

In 1917, Parker introduced a new line of jumping carry-us-alls. The horses had exaggerated poses with strong outlines and stiff attitudes showing the work of the carving machine. They were horses of great character and distinction. Parker continued making carousels until the mid-twenties. The depression right after World War I threw business off considerably, curtailing the output of the Leavenworth plant. During Parker's last years, his factory worked on a diminished scale in charge of his son Paul. Colonel Parker, a title acquired earlier, was ill eighteen months before his passing. He died at his home in Leavenworth on October 28, 1932.

The golden era of the Parker enterprises, 1912.

Parker carry-us-all, 1919.

Many carousels were sent by rail, and occasionally disaster struck. This wreck
was Pollack's portable carousel with the World at Home Show.

Henry B. Auchy

THE PHILADELPHIA TOBOGGAN COMPANY

With the success of Dentzel in Philadelphia and the mushrooming of amusement parks everywhere, there were some who felt that there was enough demand to support another factory in Philadelphia. One such person was Henry B. Auchy of Chestnut Hill. Auchy was born on January 9, 1861, at Lower Salford, Montgomery County, Pennsylvania. As a young man, Henry was in the produce business; he later branched out and founded Chestnut Hill Park, managing it successfully for its first fourteen years.

Auchy who had also gone into the liquor business, prospered and was interested in investing in the amusements. About 1899, he formed the Gray Amusement Company, using the address of his liquor establishment, 1946 Newkirk Street in Philadelphia. Louis Berni of New York, who was an importer of carousel organs, formed a corporation with himself as president and Auchy as treasurer and general manager. This firm was known as the Philadelphia Carrousel, Company, Chestnut Hill, with the specific address of each of its two officers.

Auchy's first carousel at Chestnut Hill in 1899 was a mass of jigsaw, fancy scrollwork, a zoological variety showing the Dentzel influence. But the building housing this carousel was surrounded by trees, lawns, and plenty of space on all sides.

In 1903, Henry B. Auchy and Chester E. Albright of Philadelphia established the Philadelphia Toboggan Company with the aim to "build finer and better carousels and coasters." During 1904, the Philadelphia Toboggan Company was able to build, in its factory at Germantown, five carousels, and the first was placed at Piney Beach in Virginia.

In order to produce a superior carousel, Auchy tried to secure the finest artisans. He approached Salvatore Cernigliaro, Dentzel's new carver, who had created a sensation with his astonishing carvings of cats, rabbits, goats, and other animals. He asked Cernigliaro to name his own wage. The carver, with a sense of loyalty to Dentzel who had given him a job when he arrived penniless from Italy, told Dentzel of the offer. Dentzel promised him a job for life, saying, "These new fellows are mushrooms, they can't last too long and will go out of business soon." Cernigliaro remained, and Dentzel died a few years later. The Philadelphia Toboggan Company kept making carousels for twenty-five more years.

This new carousel company built exquisitely carved carousels. The crestings were lavish; the animals showed great craftsmanship and design, and no one in the United States could match their chariots. Orders came in from Chicago, Cleveland, Los Angeles, Springfield, Rochester, Baltimore, and New Haven. The factory was kept busy producing splendid carousels and scenic rides.

The succeeding years found the firm furnishing amusement devices for many of the leading parks, controlling the interests through subsidiary holding and operating companies. In 1919, John R. Davies, Arnold Aiman, and Samuel H. High became associated with the company as stockholders and officers, all becoming active in the management.

Carousel, Euclid Beach Park, Cleveland, 1910. Built by the Philadelphia Toboggan Company.

Auchy's first carousel at Chestnut Hill, 1899.

Exterior of Chestnut Hill carousel

Carousel, Piney Beach, Virginia, 1904. Built by Philadelphia Toboggan Company.

Carousel, Vinewood Park, Topeka, Kansas, gaily decorated for the grand opening.
Built by Philadelphia Toboggan Company.

Carousel, Pabst Park, Milwaukee, Wisconsin, 1904. Built by Philadelphia Toboggan Company.

When Elitch Gardens in Denver, Colorado, wanted the Philadelphia Toboggan Company to build the finest carousel in the West, this dazzling ride was created.

Philadelphia Toboggan Exhibit at Street Railway Convention. Street Railway companies, owning many trolly parks, were excellent customers for carousels.

Riverview Park, Chicago, during the 1905–06 construction. Note the workmen preparing the building for the carousel.

Finished carousel at Riverview Park, Chicago.

Carousel, Riverside Park, Springfield, Massachusetts. Built by Philadelphia Toboggan Company.

On the way to the bank with $20,000. A great July 4th business in 1903, and a good publicity stunt for Euclid Beach Park, Cleveland. In those days, the trolly lines came right down to the popcorn and candy stands. The park, organized in 1895 by the Euclid Beach Park Company, was sold in 1901 to the Humphrey Company.

Carousel, Olympic Park, Maplewood, New Jersey. Originally made for Belle Isle Park, Detroit, in 1914. During the 1928 season, it was brought back to the Philadelphia Toboggan Company factory, reconditioned for its new owner, Henry Guenther, and erected at its present location. It may well have been the largest carousel in America. It has a sixty-foot platform diameter, eighty wooden horses, four chariots, and seated ninety-nine passengers. Larger carousels of five and six abreast were built by Stein and Goldstein of Brooklyn, but none are known to have survived.

Carousel, Los Angeles. Built by the Philadelphia Toboggan Company. Destroyed by fire in 1912.

Carousel, Luna Park, Cleveland, 1915. Chariot and crestings are typical Philadelphia Toboggan Company identification.

Paint shop at Philadelphia Toboggan Company. The primary coats have been applied in preparation for the colors and gold-leaf.

Small carousels were also made by Philadelphia Toboggan Company, but they showed none of the sophistication of the large park rides.

Carousel, Rochester, New York. Built by the Philadelphia Toboggan Company.

The Philadelphia Toboggan Company continued making carousels, installing this one at Savin Rock, New Haven, Connecticut, 1928.

William F. Mangels

WILLIAM F. MANGELS, HISTORIAN OF AMUSEMENT

Due to the growth of the amusement industry, the National Association of Amusement Parks had been organized in 1920. No man in this organization had a greater sense of the need for preserving its records and samples of past achievements than its historian, William F. Mangels.

Mangels was born in Germany in 1867, came to America at the age of sixteen, and by 1886 had an established machine shop in Coney Island, servicing many of the amusements then in operation. He took a great interest in local affairs and the history of amusement parks. Studying the United States patent records, Mangels made notes for future use. In 1907, he patented an improvement of Savage's galloping-horse action which is commonly used on all carousels today. A series of inventions followed. In 1912, he installed in Palisades Park, New Jersey, a wave-making machine for the swimming pool. In 1914, he invented and produced the "Whip" which has shaken many a happy vertebra and is made today in large and kiddy sizes.

In 1910, Mangels moved to West Fifth Street, Brooklyn, and started the production of carousels. With Marcus Charles Illions as his carver, producing the animals and ornamental woodwork, Mangels made the famous Feltman carousel at Coney Island, replacing the Looff ride, partially destroyed by fire.

The Mangels Company Carousel Works

The combination of fine carving, and strong and durable machinery earned Mangels a reputation (still true of his sons) for excellent manufacture, and his business prospered.

While Mangels was occupied in his plant, producing new and better rides, he also took a great interest in the preservation of the historical records and models of amusement devices of the past. In 1927, he proposed and organized the American Museum of Public Recreation, getting many pledges but little financial or physical support from the Association and its members. He carried on these activities practically single-handed and erected a building to house these models, artifacts, photos, and records.

For a short while, some funds were donated and the intention of maintaining a free exhibit on Surf Avenue in Coney Island almost succeeded, but Mangel's idealism alone could not support this institution. Mangels, at his own expense, housed the collection in a building next to his plant. In 1928, after the death of William H. Dentzel, Mangels interested the estate executors in donating all of the historical Dentzel tools, sign, note-marking machines, rare carved specimens, photos, and records to the Museum.

102

Looking east on Surf Avenue, Coney Island, Brooklyn, 1926. The Stubbman carousel (*right*) was built by Mangels and Illions.

Carousel, 1912. Built by Mangels.

At the age of eighty-two, Mangels wrote a book, *The Outdoor Amusement Industry*, recording the important facts which supplied a need, never-before filled. The book was sponsored by the National Association of Amusement Parks, Pools and Beaches. In 1955, Mangels, with a great desire to have the exhibits seen by the multitude, sold the contents to the Circus Hall of Fame and Horn's Cars of Yesterday, both at Sarasota, Florida. The musical instruments went to the Museum at Council Bluffs, Iowa. Mangels died on February 2, 1958 at the age of ninety-two. Some day, a plaque should be mounted—in Coney Island—to note his many contributions.

In Cincinnati, Ohio, between 1903 and 1909, three companies, all directly connected through the same management, produced some carousels. In 1903, the Queens City Carrousselle Company at 8th and Chateau, advertised its carousels. In 1906, the Gem Novelty Company at the same address advertised merry-go-rounds noting, ". . . we manufacture them from $250 to $10,000—hundreds of our machines are in operation."

A few months later, the Cincinnati Merry-Go-Round Company at Evans and South Streets inserted an ad in the Billboard, offering its wares at the lowest available prices, and in 1913, The United States Merry-Go-Round Company made its appearance in an advertisement giving 1923 Mills Avenue, Norwood, Cincinnati as its address.

George Marqua of the Gem Novelty Company and William Marqua owned the Cincinnati Merry-Go-Round Company. No carousel of major importance was ever made by any of the Cincinnati firms.

Carousel, Rocky Glen Park, Scranton, Pennsylvania, 1919. Built by Mangels.

The Dentzel Collection at the American Museum of Public Recreation, Coney Island.

Waiting for the carousel at the Great Patterson Show in Enid, Oklahoma. Under a blazing sun, 3,500 riders were accommodated in three hours.

Surf Avenue ready for the 1912 Coney Island Mardi Gras. (*Brooklyn Public Library, Photograph Collection*)

Flood at the Herman Willard Carnival

CONEY'S CHUTES AND MERRY-GO-ROUND.

Design for the 1909 Coney Island Mardi Gras Parade. The float has all the popular comic-strip characters of the day as riders.

In front of the Mangels's factory, 1909. Once a familiar sight in the city streets, the kiddie rides and local ordinances banned these small roving carousels.

Most American carousel makers made claims to being the "largest," "greatest," "finest," or "biggest." But one smaller factory in the Williamsburg section of Brooklyn wanted to be known only as the "Artistic Caroussel Manufacturers." Two of the three partners were carvers with great pride in their work.

On October 22, 1912, partnership papers were filed by Solomon Stein, Harry Goldstein, and Henry Dorber for a firm to be known as Stein, Goldstein and Dorber. Their first shop, a little three room tenement with bad lighting, was reached by going through a hallway in a wood frame building at 44 Boerum Street. There was difficulty in moving large horses after they were carved and assembled. A larger shop was then found nearby at 128 Hopkins Street. Horse-drawn wagons would back up to the shop and cart away the newly finished products for destinations all over the East. With the increase in business, the firm moved to a converted trolley-car barn at 1455–1459 Gates Avenue in Brooklyn. Henry Dorber built the machinery while Stein, Goldstein and other carvers made the horses, chariots, rims, crestings, and carved woodwork. Dorber introduced the system of using castings on the jumping horses to circumvent the Mangels sleeve patent.

Dorber left the organization in 1914. The partnership was reorganized as Stein and Goldstein, The Artistic Carousal Manufacturers. Dorber operated a carousel they had built and erected at Sheepshead Bay, Brooklyn, and later sold it to a Mr. Buck. Stein and Goldstein made huge carousels of five- and 6-abreast with sixty-foot platforms having seating capacities of seventy-two, eight-six, ninety-eight, and over one hundred. It is possible that this firm built the largest carousels ever made. Hurley's, in Boston, was huge. One of their large seventy-two-horse, four-chariot, sixty-foot-platform rides is at Oakland Beach, Rhode Island.

Murphy's carousel at Savin Rock, Connecticut is a good example of their intricate hand carving on the inner and upper panels, justifying the slogan in Stein and Goldstein's ads. Their shop made very beautiful horses and sold many singly to various makers and carousel operators. The business was dissolved after World War I.

Murphy's carousel, Savin Rock, Connecticut. (*Thomas E. McCary*)

The grand façade for the "El Dorado," created by Hugo Haase of Leipzig.

GERMAN-AMERICAN CAROUSELS

"Steeplechase, Steeplechase, the man with the funny face." So went the jingle sung by children each spring as the billposter plastered the neighborhood fences with that toothy smile that made Coney Island famous.

Steeplechase, a forty-two-acre fun palace, the largest covered amusement park in the United States also houses the most ornate, most publicized, and one of the largest carousels in America.

Before 1911, a great showpiece was brought to America, placed on Surf Avenue and Eleventh Street, Coney Island, Brooklyn, astonishing all who beheld it. But this was only the façade for the "El Dorado"—the most spectacular carousel America had ever seen. Through the carved ticket office passed amazed Americans.

The carousel, the creation of Hugo Haase of Leipzig was forty-two feet high and was a mass of carvings, fairy tale chariots—each on a different theme—and three tiers of revolving platforms, each at a different speed. From the innermost tier one entered a throne room guarded on all sides by glaring owls and life-sized angels with trumpets. At night the three spinning platforms with their carved animals reflected the lights in the eight mirrored posts topped by brilliant globes. Carved *amorini* smiled approvingly from their lofty, brilliantly colored cornices upon the couples below.

109

"El Dorado," Coney Island.

The band organ, made by Ruth und Sohn of Waldkirch, Germany, was in keeping with the front and was a staggering mass of carved figures, all tapping glockenspiels, cymbals, triangles, and drums. Its powerful tone reverberated all through Coney Island. This exhibition piece attracted huge crowds and remained here until after the Dreamland fire in May, 1911. George C. Tilyou bought the entire unit, installed the carousel inside Steeplechase, and placed the front at the Surf Avenue entrance where it served as a walkthrough to the "Barrel of Fun." A new city ordinance in 1923, creating Sixteenth Street as a public thoroughfare, forced Tilyou to move the entire front. With the exception of the ticket booth, it was found to be, not of carved wood, but made of zinc. It was cut up and, except for three lions still in use, junked.

Another naturalized American and one of the few clockwise roundabouts in America is to be found on the front lawn at Steeplechase. This roundabout with a dramatic history, now named the "Chanticleer," was once the property of Frank C. Bostock, built by Orton Sons & Spooner Ltd. It was bought in England from George Green who had named it the "Four-abreast Bantams" and then placed on the carnival grounds in Glasgow in 1910. The signs read, "Greens Galloping Chickens," "Prize Cockerells," "Prodigious Poultry," "Round 'n Round Roosters" and "Prize Bantams." While transporting it to America, the ship sank in the North Sea. Salvaging operations brought it to the surface and in 1913 landed on Tilyou's front lawn where it still crowingly turns clockwise. Up to 1924 it was still being operated by steam, but live ash from the steam center engine, landing on the wooden roof, set it on fire, destroying its charming top.

"Chanticleer," Steeplechase, Coney Island. Built by Savage of England.

Another Steeplechase ride, not a true carousel, is the altered, once competitive "Racing Derby," created by Fred Church in 1922, installed in 1924 with Illions's carved horses.

With the nationwide publicity attracted by the German-made "Eldorado," American carousel operators, hoping some of the glamor would rub off on them, announced that theirs too were German-made. The myth persists to this day and many plaques that mistakenly announce, "This carousel was hand-made in Germany and all the animals are hand-carved," must eventually come down. The impression has been handed down to present owners who do not realize the prize they possess—an American-made merry-go-round.

To help further this illusion, the band organs, which were indeed German, had names carved on their gilded façades. This was the only visible identification of manufacture. Such names as Bruder Gebrüder (Waldkirch), Ruth und Sohn (Waldkirch), and Frati (Berlin), furthered the illusion that the carousel itself was German.

111

"Galloping Chickens"

"Racing Derby"

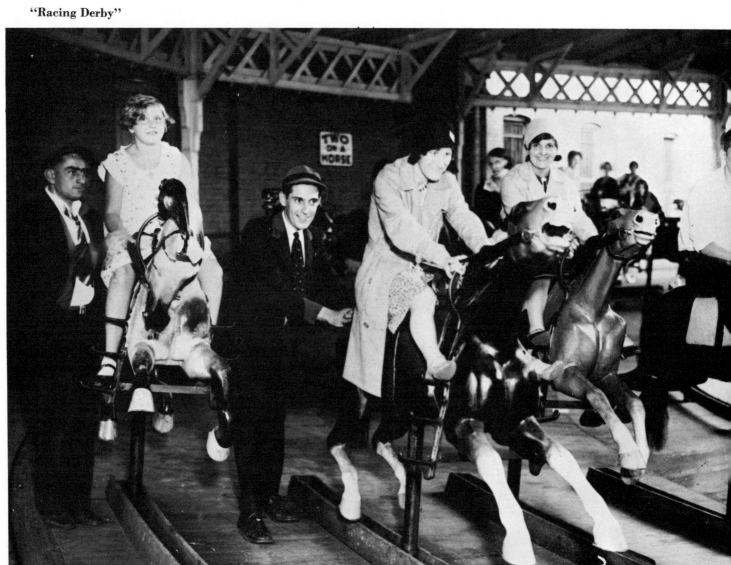

Sir Hiram Maxim's "Captive Flying Machine," 1904. (*Picture Collection, New York Public Library*)

Actually, there are very few German carousels in America and very few ever arrived on these shores. The industry in America was too strong and competitive to allow the import of rides and the tariffs and transport costs made it unprofitable.

A great many circular rides have been and are being made which are not really carousels. The most spectacular of all was Sir Hiram Maxim's "Captive Flying Machine" in 1905. It was a tall steel mast from which were suspended several blimps with seats for the lion-hearted passengers. When it was set in motion at high speed, the blimps would fly out at sixty miles per hour at spectacular heights.

Since then, many rides with names like the "Octopus," "Helicopter," "Twister," "Sky Fighter," the "Rock & Roll," the "Frolic," "Round-up," "Tilt-a-Whirl," "Flying Saucer," "Paratrooper," "Loop-a-Plane," and others with recorded music have been competing with the carousel and its band organ.

But many still sing of the glory of the carousel that is and was the most joyful of all rides. At Dorney Park, near Allentown, Pennsylvania, when the seventieth year of its operation was celebrated, Bob Plarr got out his Dad's first carousel, painted it gold and gave free rides to one and all.

The great hurricane of 1938 left the old Dentzel merry-go-round at Old Easton
Beach in this sad condition. (*Providence Sunday Journal*)

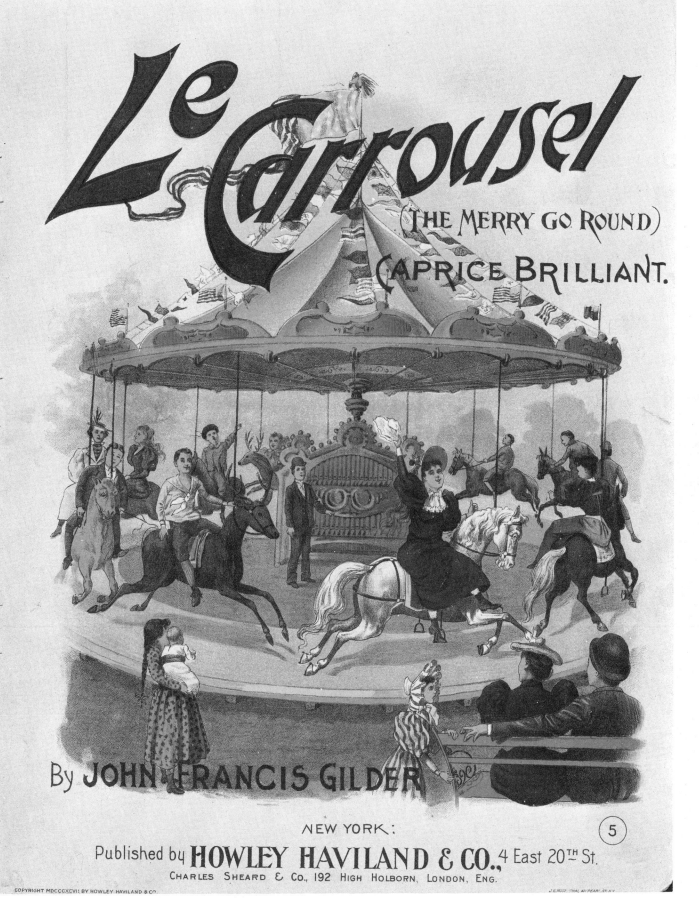

The carousel has been the theme of many songs and sonnets. In 1897 it inspired
this "Caprice Brilliant" for the piano.

Souvenir of the seventieth year of Dorney Park, Allentown, Pennsylvania.

The men who made the world go round

CHAPTER 4

AMERICAN CAROUSEL CARVERS

ONE OF THE MOST IMPORTANT PHASES OF AMERICAN CARVING, UNFORTUNATELY, HAS BEEN BY-passed by historians. Hardly anything has ever been written about our American carousel carvers and no history exists which either lists them or acknowledges their contributions to American art. One or two attempts to identify the carvers of various carousel animals has ended in pure guesswork.

The failure to index these carvers is not a willful refusal or a denigration of their contributions to American sculpture (especially in our time with its premium on folk and primitive art). Nor is the art of carousel carving too new for a proper perspective. This art dates almost as far back as ship-figurehead carving, and is as old an art as carved shop figures, and wooden Indians. It is certainly as old as circus-wagon carving, in which some of the carousel carvers excelled.

The answer lies in the unmistakable fact that little was known about them and insufficient research has yielded nothing. Records have vanished or have perished in fires and reorganizations. Books were not always kept and some of the carvers were known only by first names and approximate last names. Except in rare cases, carvings were never signed. But, much has been found in the writing of this history, which is only a beginning of a new chapter on American carousel carvers.

EARLY AMERICAN CAROUSEL SCULPTURE

"Flying Horses," and other types of early American carousels were single efforts, usually made by wheelwrights, blacksmiths, and sometimes farmers during the long winter months. At the beginning of the nineteenth century, when records show that such machines were in use, the very name indicates that there were horses on these primitive machines. No graphic record is known of these efforts. To judge from the more advanced European rides, the horses were nothing more than crude log-hacked forms approximating horses. Legs were added later, and the forms still remained crude. With the addition of horsehair manes and tails and sometimes glass eyes, the horses looked more convincing. In many cases, a general outline was marked off on wood plankings which were fastened together, and the cutting and carving came next. This may account for the strong, simple shapes found in early figures. Many had small heads, perhaps limited by the size of the planks. With the development of the carousel and the introduction of steam as a motive power, carousels took on more weight, became larger, and the carvings more refined.

Early carousel carvings developed parallel with hobby horses and rocking horses. Before 1876, carousel figures were suspended from sweeps by chains and hook marks, and hooks are sometimes found under the tail and in front of the saddle. Figures, other than horses, are known to have been used on carousels in the early nineteenth century.

Horses on the Tonawanda machines were supported from underneath by a stirrup-shaped bracket and hinge which permitted the rocking and galloping motion derived from the cone-shaped wheels underneath. Screw holes are found under the hollowed front legs, belly, and sometimes on the front of the back legs. Horses of this type were made by four factories, one as late as 1914, the earliest, about 1878.

With the development of the platform carousel about 1876, the horses and figures were supported from above by a horse rod which went through the horse, usually in front of the saddle to below the platform. These date from 1876 to the present day. Some carousel figures with a square hollowed out underneath, usually between the underneath center and front legs, were supported on a post attached to a "swinging platform." These may date from 1876 or much earlier if European. In most instances, it is impossible to distinguish a difference.

Much has been made of early, primitive "finds" and it is possible that entire rides may be stored away in old barns. A few early rides came from England and the unmistakeable resemblance of some important figures to those carved by the firm of Frederic Savage at Kings Lynn, England, in their beginning, is more than a coincidence. The merits of the carvings themselves are most important.

The term "primitive" is generally used to designate unschooled, crude, naive, or unsophisticated art. Most of our carousel carvers were unschooled in sculpture, naive and unsophisticated in their art understanding. But it can hardly be said that theirs was a "primitive art," nor because of its large commercial use, can their art be termed "folk art." Actually, theirs was a straightforward statement with a primary concern for the elemental. Nor were there any signs of crudeness in the products of the carousel manufacturers after the 1900 period. Oddities did crop up now and then such as the attachment of a full three-dimensional Indian head to the pommel of a saddle—which is in a category by itself.

Strange devices were often used to attract attention and send the childish imagination soaring. A horse ready for a dress parade might, for example, be equipped with a mace, sword, and shield, and a bunch of wild roses along a cropped mane. An armored horse may have had twenty or thirty colored glass ornaments set on its flanks. Saddle pads of others were the skins of wild beasts, usually with the head peering out from under the back of the saddle. The whole was not unlike the decorations employed by the *Escadron des Turcs* commanded by the Prince de Condé in the grand Carrousel of 1662.

American sculpture, in its functional form—circus, carnival, and carousel—ranges from the classical to the primitive, the rococo to the un-named. American carousel carvers tried to be as representational as possible. Each had to say quickly and with convincing detail, "this is an Indian's horse," "this is a cavalryman's horse," "this horse is an armored horse for a knight of the round table," or "this is a huntsman's horse," or of course, this is a "cowboy's horse." Or if you liked the circus or the barnyard, there were animals of all kinds to carry you away into these.

The carver, with the great advance of the carousel, had to make his wood sculpture a sturdy beast that could hold up hundreds of riders in one day and perform this service under an

118

exposure which hardly any other piece of sculpture could possibly endure. Many of these carousels were demountable, and like the carnival, played one-day stands. The entire carousel was knocked down, put on wagons, and erected again in the next town. The wooden horses held up admirably. However, not many survived, and the few that did are regarded with great respect.

There were not too many carvers of carousel figures and it was possible for one carver with a pantographic cutting apparatus to turn out a vast amount of woodwork in one year. This process was in general practice after 1910. In North Tonawanda, the carving machine was first used in 1913. After the figures came off the machine, it was necessary for carvers to chisel out the details and hand carve the important features. Legs, tails, and some bodies were mass produced. Heads and chariots were almost always hand carved. Crestings at first were all hand made, later, cast from molds.

Band organ façades were made by some of the American carousel manufacturers. Usually, the organ was purchased abroad or from the few makers in America, and the factory's carvers would make façades of their own design. This was not a common practice. It was more usual for the organ to be imported, with the façade bearing the carousel maker's name painted on or carved at the source of supply. These façades have a great deal of the circus-carving charm. Many had figures with movable parts that beat some percussion instrument, turned their bodies, and moved their heads.

CARVERS AND MANUFACTURERS

Several of our carousel makers were also carvers. Of these, the earliest known is Charles I. D. Looff. Looff made his first three carousels without assistance, his first erected in 1876 at Coney Island, Brooklyn. Trained as a woodcarver in Schleswig-Holstein (then a Danish province) he came to America, settled in Brooklyn where he worked in a furniture factory during the day and carved his carousel figures in his spare time at home.

With the success of his first carousel at Coney Island in 1876, another in 1880, and an Atlantic City carousel a few years later, Looff felt confident to employ others and opened his shop at 30–37 Bedford Avenue, Brooklyn. (A short distance away from his new carousel factory was the shop of Samuel A. Robb who made "ship and steamboat carvings, eagles, scrolls, block letters, figure carving, tobacconist signs, dentist, and druggist signs.") By 1890, Looff had four carvers working with him. Later, his son Charles Looff, Jr. worked in the shop designing many of the saddle packs on the Looff horses. Looff, Sr., was a splendid carver and even his first carousel at Coney Island had figures that were well carved, although quaint.

Looff had a large picture of George Washington astride his favorite horse which he used as his model. Most of his horses were gentle-seeming creatures. They were jolly, with bulging nostriles to show heavy breathing and many had teeth exposed in a smile. Looff used a rosette on the breast of his animals and the saddle pad was decorated with tassels and glass ornaments of different colors. (His etched glass and mirrors were purchased from J. R. Donnelly Company of Classon Street, Brooklyn.) Looff's lumber was bought from William Breen's Sons at 24 Greenpoint Avenue. (Whitewood planking of 2½ inches cost six cents a foot in 1905.) Looff used a limited number of poses, varying the saddle decorations, trappings, and colors. Real horse-hair tails of full length were used.

Lions, tigers, panthers in pairs pulling small chariots; camels, zebras, greyhounds of large and beautiful proportions, storks, ostrich, deer, and other animals were also carved by Looff. The rims and crestings were usually painted panels on tin or zinc. With time, especially near the seashore, the paint all peeled and flaked.

In 1909, Looff carved a fine carousel of fifty-four horses which he presented to his daughter, Emma Looff Vogel, as a wedding present. After this date, it is doubtful if Looff did much of his own carvings. He had several large holdings requiring his full time in administration.

119

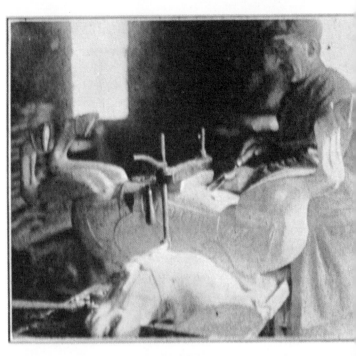

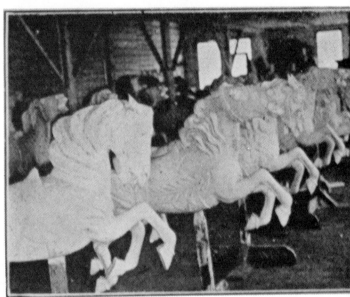

The Spillman Engineering Corporation works (*left to right*): Ben Heim building the body, Bill Jagow carving the body, C. F. Kopp carving heads, and the horse ready for the paint shop.

120

His factory, moved from Greenpoint to Riverside, was only one of these. In 1910 he moved to Ocean Park, California, installing several large carousels on the West Coast, keeping active until his death in 1918. His style of carving influenced other carousel makers. Looff, doubtlessly, was the first of America's great carousel carvers.

North Tonawanda, the "Lumber City," was a magnet for woodworkers and carvers. In 1883, the Tonawanda steam carousel that by wheels moved on a circular track was introduced. Within ten years, a large number of these found their way throughout the North and South American continents. The horses were hinged on supports fastened to the platform. Since there was no centerpole, there was no need for overhead support, the galloping action resulting from eccentrics under the platform.

The horses had a folksy appearance, probably influenced by Looff. Ears upright, slightly forward, puffy nostrils, a slight smile and eager look, parted forelock, brushed mane, rolling to the right, a simple cavalry saddle, usually nailed on afterwards, sometimes with an eagle motif at the back, a fringed and checkered saddle blanket and a spare amount of carving were standard. The legs were stiff and squarish, the body box-like. Poses were limited to either a galloping or jumping action. These horses were typical of the many made by the Armitage Herschell Company and later by the Herschell-Spillman Company and with but few changes continued until 1915.

In the course of future reorganizations of the Armitage Herschell, Spillman-Herschell, Allan Herschell and the Spillman Engineering Corporation, almost all of the early carvers, still alive, were kept on. They continued as before, showing more sophistication in the carving and finally produced figures with life-like realism.

A contemporary description of the Spillman carving shop notes:

The carving shop is just above the carpenter shop. Bodies, legs, heads, tails of the different animals are piled about in orderly profusion; also parts of chariots, shields and cornices, all of which are hand-carved and very beautiful. One of my first impressions of detail was the discovery that each foot of the marvelously natural little horses, was shod with a real horseshoe.

Next on our route was the store room, where horses, lions, tigers, ostriches, frogs, dogs, cats, deer, camels and swans were arranged in racks, carefully curtained in sections and covered to protect from dust.

SALVATORE CERNIGLIARO

Gustav A. Dentzel, America's pioneer carousel builder made rapid progress in the development of the carousel. A centerpole from which eight arms held small park bench seats attached by a chain, soon gave way to carved horses. Dentzel, a skilled woodworker, no doubt made the first set of horses himself. As the volume of the business increased, the carving shop became a busy place and the racks were filled with wooden animals waiting for the finishing strokes of the chisel.

In 1903, a striking change took place in the Dentzel carvings. Salvatore Cernigliaro, an Italian immigrant, landed on these shores. His own story (from a letter to the author) follows:

In October, 1902, I landed here in the United State as immigrant. I was alone with few coins in pocket, 23 years old, healthy and a very, very strong boy full of energy and *corragio*. I was coming from Palermo, Italy; my trade was wood-carver in furniture. The first job I got in Philadelphia was with a Mr. Morris, a wealthy man who manufactured red merry-go-round, not for sale but for his own use, or his own parks. It was a new job for me carving wood horses for merry-go-round as I was carver for furniture. But I didn't get lost. Very quickly I got acquainted with the new work and I like it very much. After three months, summer came, Mr. Morris closed his shop and opened his park so I was out of work. I asked somebody if there was any other carousel shop in Philadelphia. They told me of Mr. Dentzel's shop in Germantown near Erie Avenue.

I managed to find the place. Facing Germantown Avenue was Mr. Dentzel's house where he lived

In this 1894 photograph of the Dentzel carving shop, Gustav A. Dentzel (*second from right*) stands behind the painted giraffe. Edward P. Dentzel, Gustav's second son (*extreme left*), William H. Dentzel, who succeeded his father in business (*fourth from left*). Bill carved the figure after it was assembled. In the back row, with the beard, is Leopold Ross who carved only the bodies and legs. The carver to Bill's left is unidentified. With glasses is Gustav's brother, Henry, who assembled the wooden bodies (*sixth from left*).

. . . inside a large yard was a little factory. When I entered the yard, Mr. Dentzel was in front of the house and stopped me. That time, I couldn't speak English—only I could say three words—me woodcarver, job? Mr. Dentzel noticed I was an immigrant and talked to me in German which I couldn't understand. I understood there was no job for me and I walked away. After one week, I was still out of work. It happened that I was still around for any job and I found myself near Mr. Dentzel's shop and one block from the shop where is St. Stefano church. I went into the church and I pray. I said, Mr. Lord, I have only $4.00 in my pocket—it is my last pay for my board and if I don't find job now, they will throw me out. It was a hot day and I was very very thirsty. I remembered that in the middle of the Dentzel yard was an artesian well. When I got there, again Mr. Dentzel was in front of his house. He recognized me and started again to talk in German. Again I repeated my three words— me woodcarver, job? Mr. Dentzel was a good man and feel pity for poor immigrant, so he motion me to follow him. Inside shop, there was a very good woodcarver, Mr. Boory, a Tyrolean, who could speak a few Italian words. He told me that Mr. Dentzel one week ago, gave me job but I didn't come, I said I didn't understand him. He told me to bring my tools and start work immediately. I went out of the shop to St. Stefano church and I thank Lord.

122

"Cherni," as he was later called, threw out the old formulas of carving by pre-set patterns and caused a furor. However, his carvings showed such originality that Mr. Dentzel permitted him to continue and announced his decision to the shop.

Cherni introduced the fancy straps, elaborate drapery, horses garlanded with flowers, the Dentzel cat, bunny, and pig. After the death of Gustav Dentzel in 1909, the factory was closed until the estate was settled. When it reopened, William H. Dentzel, who had worked with his father, took over and re-employed Albert and Daniel Muller who had left a few years before to organize their own factory. Both were excellent carvers and the entire carving staff was turning out very spirited and realistic animals. The 1922 catalogue shows little change from the earlier carvings and until the death of William H. Dentzel in 1928 and the closing of the factory, very few innovations were made. Mr. Cherni is still alive and at the age of eighty-four teaches art in California.

Salvatore Cernigliaro (*Jack Fried*)

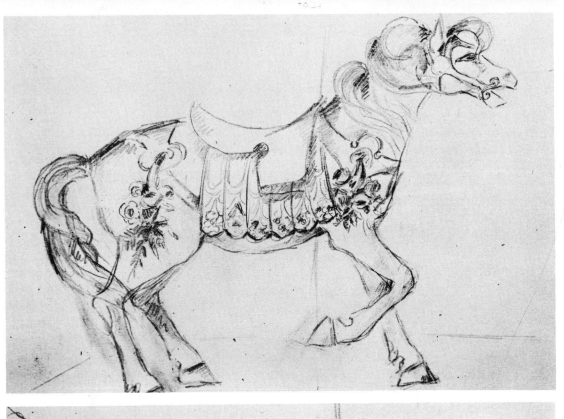

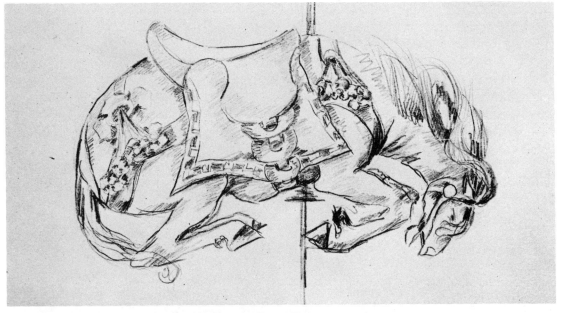

From the first sketch book of Salvatore Cernigliaro

One of the last and also one of America's greatest carousel carvers was Marcus Charles Illions. Born in 1866 in Vilna, Poland, Illions at the age of eight ran away from an apprenticeship as a woodcarver, sojourned in Germany and later made his way to England. He found employment at Savage's where he developed into a first-rate carver, making roundabout animals, wagon fronts, and circus carvings. Illions was taken by Frank C. Bostock of the wild animal shows to the United States to finish the wagon carvings which Illions had started in England.

Illions had a shop at 747 Dean Street, Brooklyn. In the first Brooklyn directory listing he appears 1897–98 as Michael Ilion, carver. Illions's catalogue gives the 1892 date for his first American establishment. In 1903–4 he is listed as Marcus C. Illions, carver, New Pier Wk, Coney Island. At the time of the first listing, Illions was already engaged in carousel carving also listing, "Show Fronts," "Hand Sculptured Horses," "Circus Wagons," and "Highest Class Carousells." His partner, Theodore Hunger, a blacksmith, made the mechanical parts while Illions made all the horses, chariots, and decorative work. The firm was later dissolved, but Illions continued his carving business. At the time that Luna Park was going up, Illions reached wide fame with his flamboyant carvings and imaginative creations of scroll work. The wooden-chariot ticket offices he carved for Thompson and Dundy, the owners, were placed at the entrance of Luna Park, bringing Illions great publicity.

About 1909, Illions moved to 2739 Ocean Parkway, Coney Island, where he established a large carving shop. Here, he carved carousel animals, chariots, crestings, ticket booths, organ fronts, circus-wagon fronts and cashier wagons. Illions was a superb draftsman. Little is known of his early education, but his work shows that he had an intimate knowledge of Greek and Roman sculpture, as well as the classic arts. Like a number of his fellow carvers, he also did various types of carving for synagogues. One of his most notable works is the "Lion of Judah," which he donated and until recently was over the ark bearing the torah at the Seabreeze Avenue synagogue.

Illions designed his entire animal, first making a careful drawing. This was then transferred to a large cardboard sheet and used as a form for cutting blocks of whitewood. Illions employed mainly members of his family, in the tradition of the Renaissance craftsmen. But only Illions carved the heads. When busy, Illions had relatives come in to help out. Cousin Harry and nephew Phil Seskin painted the horses, first applying a coat of flat white lead. When dry, they did a masterly job of applying the Japan colors and gold leaf, preserved with a coat of spar varnish. Every inch of work was under the supervision of the "master" who seemed to "pop in every minute to look it over." Another relative, Jake Illions, came in to help out when the orders were especially heavy.

About 1916, Illions teamed up with William F. Mangels and moved his shop over the Mangels factory on West Eighth Street, Coney Island. Illions made all the carved and wood work and Mangels made all the metal parts, centerpoles, and mechanical apparatus. Together, they produced some of the most notable carousels, each the perfectionist in his own field. One of these was the Feltman carousel at Coney Island. The fancy floral scroll carving was an Illions's trademark.

Both Mangels and Illions were men of strong wills and personalities who respected each other. However, this relationship did not last very long and Illions again went his separate way. He continued his work, still using the Mangels factory for his mechanical supplies. Organized as M. C. Illions and Sons Inc. Carousell Works, he made six types of carousels—Supreme, Superior, Superb, and Monarch I, II, and III. The Supreme had a fifty-four-foot platform, four abreast, seventy-four horses and two large chariots "sculptured by hand in the Rococo and Louis XV styles." (The wording was Illions's.) The Superior with a fifty-foot platform had sixty-six horses, two sculptured dragon chariots, seating altogether seventy-four

The carving shop of Marcus Charles Illions. Illions in traditional white carver's apron stands behind his son, Rudy at right.

Illions's Luna Park chariot

Some of America's greatest carnival carvings were destroyed in the fire that started on a cold, windy winter's day in December, 1911. Luna Park was wiped out, built up again, had several more fires, and finally in 1946 a fire destroyed the park forever. A large housing development now occupies the site. (*Brooklyn Public Library, Photograph Collection*)

Feltman carousel at Coney Island

passengers but with a carrying capacity of 250. Illions's portable carousels had the same fancy carved work on a smaller scale.

There were as many as four Illions carousels operating in Coney Island at one time and a great many scattered throughout the East. Two of the Coney Island carousels are still operating, owned by McCullough. Illions also carved the horses for the Steeplechase and other racecourse rides.

Illions knew horses. He maintained a stable and was a familiar figure each dawn galloping down the bridle path along Ocean Parkway. His style of carving, influenced by his training in England, bears a resemblance to the carvings of Anderson of Bristol. Illions, however, used the Arabian steed as his model, as well as the mustang and quarter horse, imparting a great action and sensitivity to his animals. His style was copied by nearly all carousel carvers and many of his innovations and characteristics are found in the makes of others.

Joseph L. Carrolo, now eighty-six years old, who worked for Charles Looff, tells of Looff speaking of Illions with envy and remarking, "Of the horse carvers, Mike Illions is kingpin." None of the happy and sweet characteristics of Looff's early smiling horses show in Illions's work. Illions's were unmanageable steeds, straining at the bit, manes tossed angrily about, legs tense, ready to dash at the crack of the guns, with bodies strong enough to carry the most active child or heavy adult. In his later years, Illions anticipated Henry Moore's molded space by carving large openings with interesting negative patterns in the tossed manes of his wooden steeds.

During the depression of 1928, the entire carousel-making business came to a halt and its carvers were thrown out of work. Illions became impoverished and did mainly repair work on old carousels, carving new legs and replacing broken parts. At this time he used the Long

Island Depot building at Manhattan Beach as his shop and living quarters. His sons scattered throughout the country and found employment in the amusement business. The master died at the age of seventy-eight on August 11, 1949 and is buried in Washington Cemetery in Brooklyn. At his head is a simple, uncarved stone.

OTHER CARVERS

In March, 1899, the *New York Times* was sufficiently impressed with the production of the New York Carousal Manufacturing Company in Brooklyn to send a reporter and photographer to their factory. The reporter wrote that, "25 carvers are kept at work all year round." While it is unlikely that twenty-five carvers were always kept busy in C. W. F. Dare's carving shop, except in this case to furnish the horses for Tilyou's rides, it is more probable that a much smaller number were employed in making carousl horses and figures.

Brooklyn—the borough of churchs, carousels, and carousel carvers—had still another carver at 202 Ocean Parkway, not too far from Prospect Park. Charles Carmel's carving shop was right near the bridle path and riding stables. If models of horses were needed, Carmel had simply to open his two front doors and take his choice. Several of the carousel makers called on Carmel for carved horses, legs, tails, and other parts. Fred Dolle and William F. Mangels bought his horses as well as Murphy and others from about 1910 to 1918.

THE PARKER HORSES

From the mid-nineties to about 1915, Charles W. Parker's horses were unmistakenly Parker creations. With his new line in 1917, the identification became even stronger.

Some early Parker horses were in a class by themselves. They were long sinewy creatures with long leg muscles carved in interesting shapes. Their heads were thin, long, and sensitive;

Parker's carvers, Eugene Drisco (*left*) and Leon White (*right*).

their manes rolled back in gentle "S" curves and forelocks flowed back under the ears following the contours of the head. Parker had many skilled carvers, engaged in making huge carved show-fronts, wagons, wagon-fronts, and carousel horses.

Poplar wood was mainly used. Before 1900, most of the fronts, horses, and crestings were hand carved. Cutting machines were then used, and like his Eastern counterparts, Parker had most of the horses machine cut and hand finished. There is no record of Parker making any other carousel animal than the horse.

In 1917, Parker copyrighted the designs of a new set of horses for his carry-us-alls. The horses, smallish in size, were long stretchy animals, with definite strong silhouettes in similar negative patterns. They looked machine cut. They were smaller than previous designs and painted in very vivid pastel colors, sprayed on with an air brush, and glossed with a heavy coat of spar varnish. Since all of Parker's carry-us-alls with but four exceptions, were made for portability, these had to be designed so that the horses could be stacked one on another on the transport. Like all other makes, Parker's horses had hollow heads and necks; and laminated bodies. Tails and legs were solid.

About the 1917 period, when all the Parker designs underwent changes, he mentioned that he "imported" carvers to do his work on organ fronts, wagon fronts, and others. After this period, the styles went unchanged and became standard thereafter. Parker horses and carousels were not too frequently found in the East.

THE PHILADELPHIA TOBOGGAN COMPANY HORSES—AND OTHERS

The Philadelphia Toboggan Company's first carver, John Zalar, was brought from New York by Messrs. Berni and Auchy to set the styles and carve the figures and chariots. The chariots and horses were among the finest made. Most were classic in appearance with some crudities which did not affect the overall impression. Not much is remembered about this carver. He had tuberculosis and was ordered by his doctor to "go west." In California, he carved horses, sending them east to the factory, for only a short time. About 1911, the horses took on an odd look—long heads, eyes too high and too close, awkward stances with no feeling for equine anatomy. The knees were round, legs curved with improbable joints, and the total effect was an odd animal.

About 1912 the styles changed and from 1924 remained fairly well fixed until the early 1930's. This change was due to the hiring of a carver, who like so many others, got his start in a furniture factory. Frank Carretta was born in Milan, Italy, came to America as a youth and was employed in a furniture factory in Philadelphia. He learned the trade of furniture carving but disliked it. He had tried his hand at carousel carving. On learning that Auchy was looking for carvers, he applied, was hired at once and within twelve months became the carving foreman, making new patterns, carving the heads, bodies, and chariots himself. Like Illions, Carretta was a perfectionist.

At the National Amusement Park conventions, during the late 1920's, one of the features was a carving contest among the various factories. From the few that entered. Carretta won in 1928 with a dappled charger with a huge tossed mane. In 1929, he won with a medieval palfrey with fancy trappings. Carretta remained with the company until the reorganization. His carvings were outstanding works of sculpture, earning him a niche in the carousel-carvers Hall of Fame, Sarasota, Florida.

In a little shop in Brooklyn, in a neighborhood bordered on one side by pushcarts and stalls with their shawled and bearded peddlers and on the other by the crowded tenements teeming with newly-arrived immigrants from Eastern Europe, were two excellent wood carvers, Solomon Stein and Harry Goldstein. Like their neighbors, they too had come to America, where the "streets were paved with gold and one could walk free and equal with no fear of

130

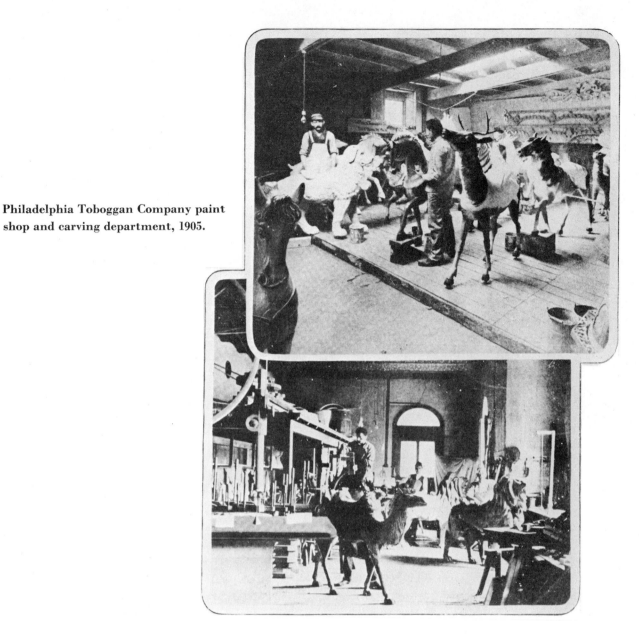

Philadelphia Toboggan Company paint shop and carving department, 1905.

pogroms." Like the others, they also found out that to make a living, one had to work from early dawn to dusk. And if you walked in groups, the Marcy Avenue hoodlums wouldn't harm you.

Each man started individually, as a carver of ladies wooden combs, which were then in vogue. In a crowded little shop, carving these fancy combs, were other carvers. 1906 was a year in which new enterprises were being established in Coney Island. The merry-go-rounds and the fairy-tale towers of Luna Park were objects of great attraction and the carvings of Illions gave pride to his countrymen, who thought they too could make such things—"a comb is smaller and harder to carve."

Sol Stein and Harry Goldstein decided to carve a merry-go-round horse and came up with a better than passable example. Excited by their success, they decided to make carousels, first making single horses and selling them. It was not until 1912, when they had found Henry Dorber, who had experience with carousels, and could build all the machinery needed, that they set up their carousel factory, moving from their cramped tenement shop to 128 Hopkins Street in Brooklyn.

131

Philadelphia Toboggan Company carving department, 1925.

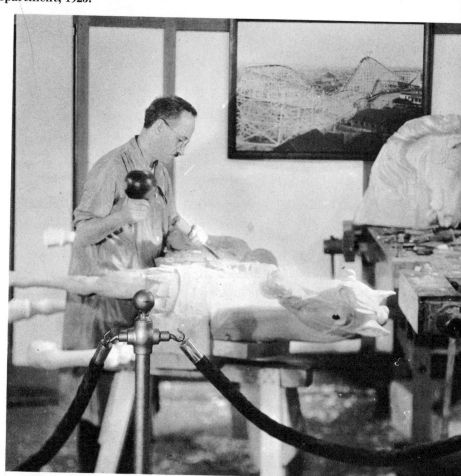

Carretta carving at the 1927 National Amusement Park convention

132

Several of the comb carvers, who also carved patterns for plaster architectural molds, joined the organization. The business grew rapidly, forcing them to expand. They moved to a converted car barn on Gates Avenue, Brooklyn, and became engaged in large productions. In the December 22, 1917 issue of the *Billboard*, they advertised, "3 to 6 abreast jumping horse carousels." No other firm made such huge machines, either in the United States or abroad. They also undertook the carving of circus wagons and carved fronts. Opinion seemed unanimous that they lived up to their advertisements as "the Artistic Caroussel Manufacturers."

Goldstein was restless at the carver's bench, rocking back and forth as he carved away. Stein was very quiet, worked quickly, and with authority. Stein and Goldstein carved the heads, leaving the other parts of the wooden anatomy to their other carvers. The horses were huge—scaled up—and flowers were found along the neckline, pommel of the saddle, and almost anywhere else for effect. Each carousel had a king's horse or an armored horse and two or more fine chariots. In spite of the profusion of flowers and delicate scroll carvings, the horses were wild-looking and like a painting then in favor, "The Horse Fair," by Rosa Bonheur; the total effect was overwhelming. The rims, mirror frames, chariots, and other decorative woodwork was a mass of intricate, delicate and gold-leafed carvings, revealing their comb-carving training.

Mass production in the mid-twentieth century started to replace the handwork of the carvers. High operation costs and the lack of skilled carvers to replace those deceased brought new methods of manufacturing horses for the modern carousels. The age of plastics and prefabricated aluminum steeds will make many a romanticist reflect nostalgically upon the era that produced fine carvings and stables of stately wooden steeds.

Assembling bodies at the Allan Herschell Company.

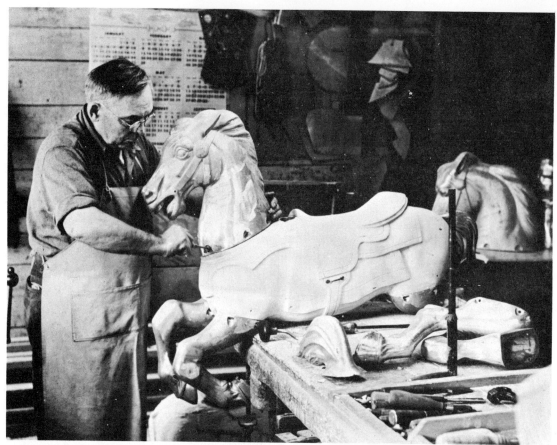

Metal parts. Allan Herschell Company.

The carving machine. Allan Herschell Company.

Painting the horses. Allan Herschell Company.

CHAPTER 5

CAROUSEL ANIMALS, FIGURES, CHARIOTS, CARVINGS, CRESTINGS, AND MACHINES

ALMOST EVERY CONCEIVABLE CREATURE TO BE FOUND IN NOAH'S ARK (AND SOME NOT TO BE found there) were made by the carousel carvers.

From England came serpents, dragons bearing chariots, and Hieronymous Bosch creatures being crushed by the chariot wheels, ostriches, peacocks, cockerels, bears, boars, pigs, lions, mermaids, and centaurs garbed in uniforms of the Boer war decked with three rows of medals. Some of these were portraits of the war's heroes. From Germany came horses with large heads and shortened backs, festooned with mirrored ornaments, cut glass, and decorative trimmings and also, bears, tigers, donkeys, lions, birds, and others. From France, simple cows, donkeys, pigs, hens, rhinoceros, and others. And American carvers, not to be outdone, made Arabian steeds, mustangs, quarter horses, ponies, donkeys, frogs, goats, lions, tigers, birds, roosters, hens, camels, kangaroos, buffaloes, giraffes, dogs, cats, cows, rabbits, storks, zebras, elephants, fish, ostriches, swans, bears, pigs, and chariots sporting the American eagle with spread wings guarding the flight of the never-ending circle.

There were animals that moved up and down and swayed and some with movable tongues, heads, or other parts. Some emitted sounds only to be overwhelmed by the volume of the band organ. But it was found that the children always chose a horse to ride. The dappled gray was the favorite and the armored horse came next. Some of the other creatures frightened the children, and most of these were discontinued after the late 1920's.

There have also been single efforts by unschooled carvers who have made entire carousels or individual figures with the purpose of creating a group for an entire ride. Some such figures have been found in unfinished condition with legs or tails missing. Some carvings from early carousels have found their way into private collections and folk art museums. The origin of most of these is unknown. However, this is no deterrent to those who recognize the importance of these figures and their native charm. This is one form of Americana that is still available at relatively small cost. Each passing day, the supply diminishes and shortly they will be as rare as ships' carvings.

THE WIDE WORLD OF CAROUSEL SCULPTURE

Belgian and English

Ancient carousel figure, Belgian, sixteenth century.

Saddle detail, 1910. (*Eric Brown*)

Two roundabout horses, *ca.* 1900. (*Eric Brown*)

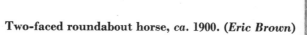
Two-faced roundabout horse, *ca.* 1900. (*Eric Brown*)

Centaur, made by Savage's Ltd. England 1905 (Author's collection)

Dragons, *ca.* 1900. (*Eric Brown*)

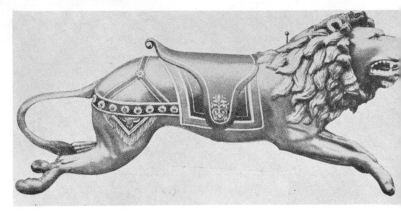

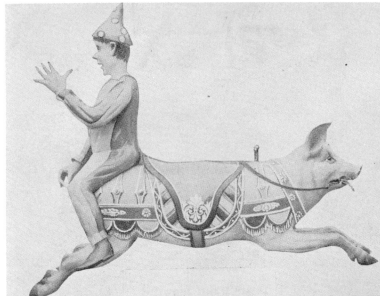

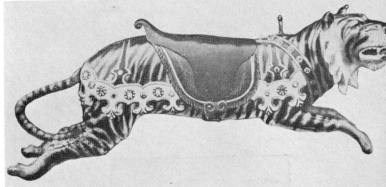

Three German pieces, a lion, pig, and tiger.

Lion, 1839, German. Made by Michael Dentzel.

Lion and tiger and single tiger, 1911. Made by Joseph Hübner and F. Heyn, Neustadt, Germany. (Swenson Collection)

Horse, 1911. Made by Friedrich Heyn, Germany

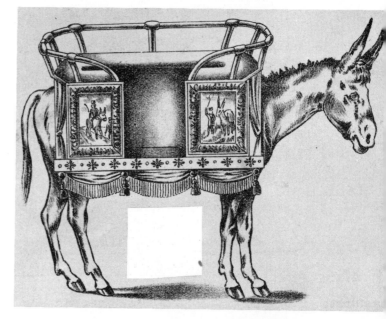

Group, 1911. Made by Hübner-Bothmann-Heyn, Germany.

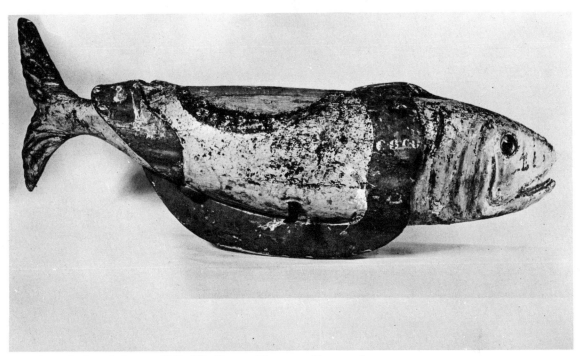

"Coco," the whale, *ca.* **1880. (Shelburne Museum, Vermont)**

Horse, *ca.* **1880. (Watch Hill, Rhode Island)**

Peacock, ca. 1900. (New York Historical Assn.) Donkey and Horse, ca. 1885.
(Swenson Collection)

Camel and Lioness, *ca.* 1885. (Stony Point Folk Art Gallery)

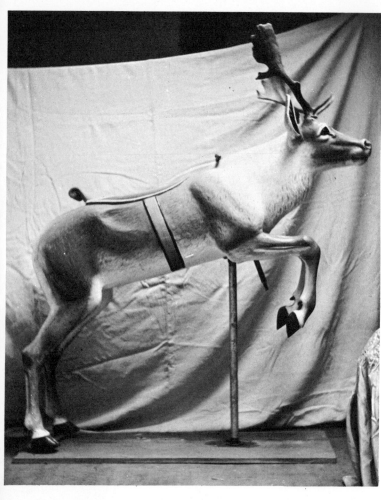

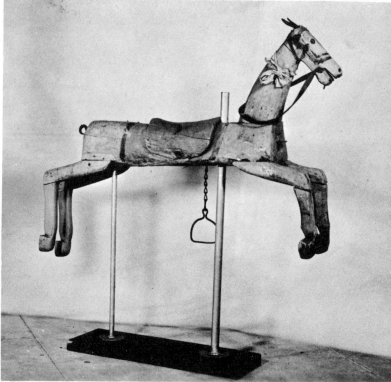

Elk, 1910. (Swenson Collection)

Rooster, *ca.* 1885. (Index of American Design)

Horse, 1879. Made by Carl Landow.

Horse and Lion, 1878. (C. W. F. Dare catalogue)

Horse, *ca.* 1888. (George Breckner, Jr. Collection)

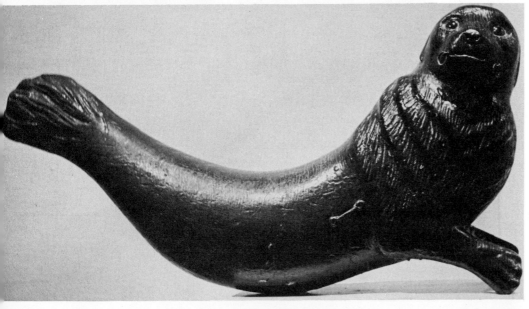

Seal (Swenson Collection)

Cat with fish, *ca.* **1903. Made by Cernigliaro (Author's carousel)**

Flirting rabbit and goat, *ca.* 1903 (Author's carousel). Carved by Cernigliaro.

149

Horse, *ca.* 1888. (State Historical Society of Wisconsin)

Rooster, *ca.* 1902. (Stony Point Folk Art Gallery)

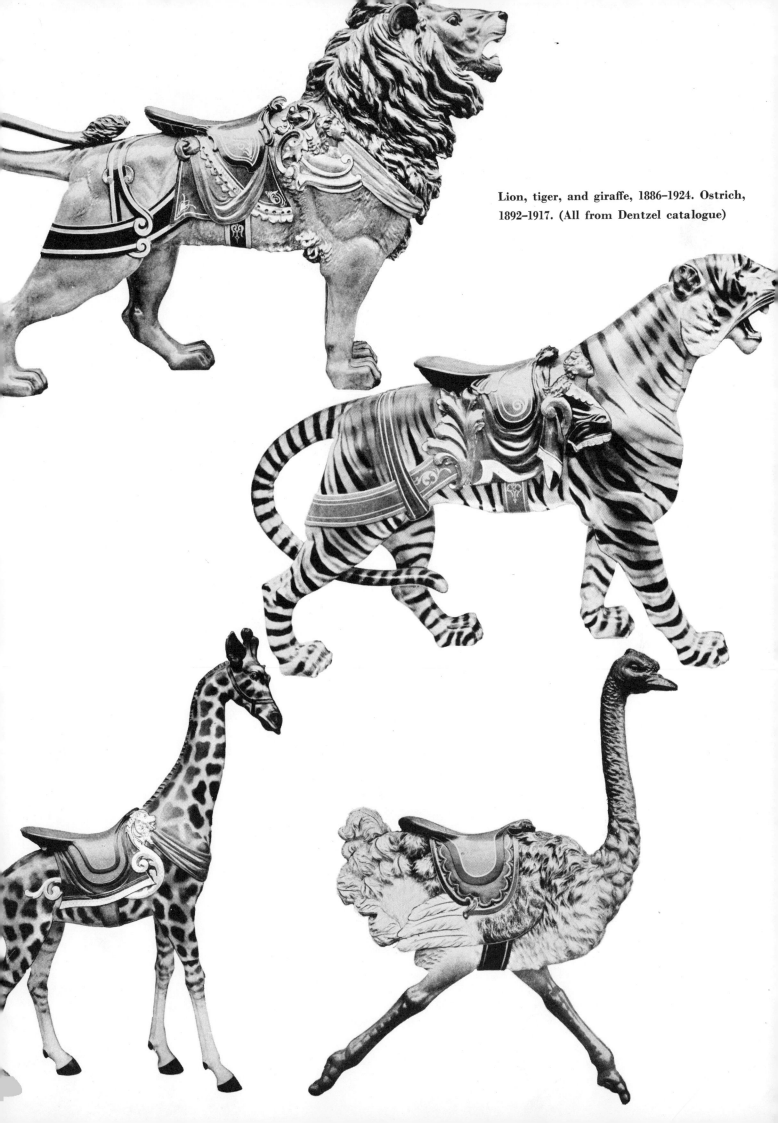

Lion, tiger, and giraffe, 1886–1924. Ostrich, 1892–1917. (All from Dentzel catalogue)

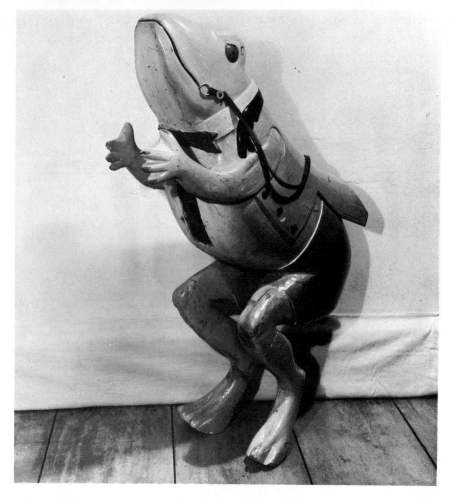

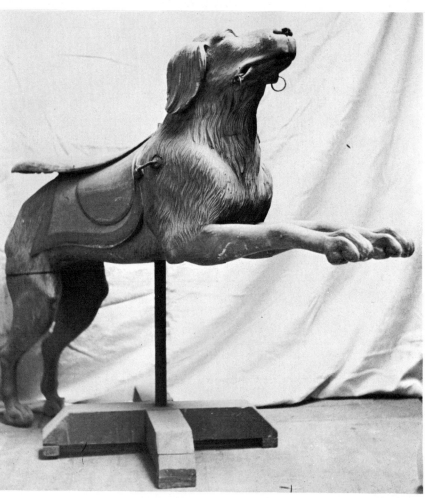

Frog and dog, 1924. Made by the Spillman Engineering Corporation. (Dog in Swenson Collection, frog in Biehler-Coger Collection.)

Horse, 1912. Signed by Illions (including a self portrait).

From Illions's album of his own work, 1912.

Sea monster, horse, and lion, 1905. (Philadelphia Toboggan Company catalogue)
carved by John Zalar.

Horses, 1911. (Philadelphia Toboggan Company Album)

Horse, 1911. Made by the Philadelphia Toboggan Company.

Silver Anniversary Horse, 1928. Made by the Philadelphia Toboggan Company. Carved by Frank Carretta.

Elephant, 1915. Made by the Allan Herschell Company.

Horses, 1924. Made by the Spillman Engineering Corporation.

Horses, 1910. Made by C. W. Parker. (Swenson Collection)

161

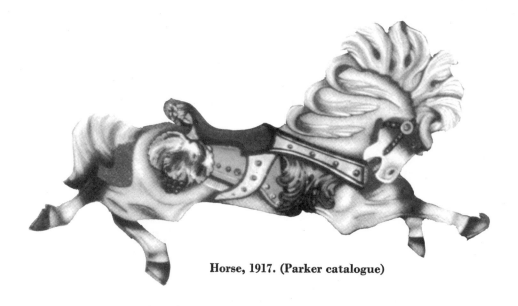

Horse, 1917. (Parker catalogue)

The Swenson Collection

162

Chariots as used on carousels were also called gondolas, boats, cars, Lohengrins, carriages, cabs, and swing bodies. Most often they were fastened to the carousel, and their main use was for those either too young or too old to mount a horse.

Some chariots were simply covered benches with only the outward sideboard carved, the inner cut to follow the outward contour. Carved in relief, the themes ranged from St. George's dragon to characters from children's books.

Early chariots made by C. W. F. Dare in 1878 seated two. They were suspended from above, rocking with the ride, becoming very rocky at the stopping of the carousel.

Philadelphia Toboggan chariots were among the finest made in America. With the exception of Illions, nobody could match the conception and carvings of these fine showpieces. No two were exactly alike. The Columbia theme, the eagle, lovers, and combinations of these were recurringly found on their chariots. The horses, in pairs, had saddles for riders, and in 1926, some were converted to jumpers, rare for chariot horses.

Illions made very fancy chariots in the Rococo and Louis XV styles but only for large and specially-ordered carousels. For the medium-sized carousel other chariots or variations with more monstrous and frightening wheels were made. It was Illions's Luna Park cashier chariots that started the idea for their use on carousels.

Parker also made dragon chariots as well as folk-theme cabs for his carry-us-alls. Often they featured a biting battle between a dragon and a python.

CRESTINGS

The upper decorative outside parts of the carousel, referred to by some manufacturers as the "crestings" are also called the rims, cornices, or shields, and known to the English as the "rounding-boards." Some had carved frames surrounding mirrors or painted panels whose subjects varied from the sublime to the ridiculous. Some were painted by skilled artists who thus showed their European training, others were naive. Many American rims were carved, others cast in a composition plaster. Almost all English rounding-boards were carved wood.

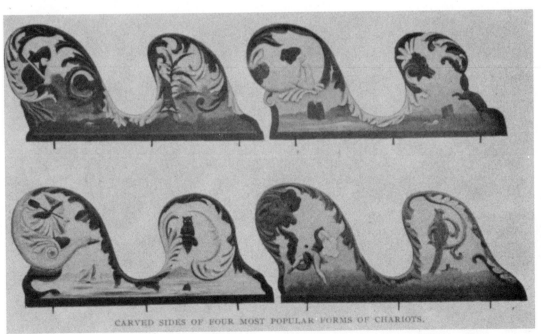

CARVED SIDES OF FOUR MOST POPULAR FORMS OF CHARIOTS.

Herschell-Spillman chariots, 1905, featuring Robinson Crusoe (*top left*), The Mermaid (*top right*), Mother Goose (*bottom left*), and Sinbad the Sailor (*bottom right*).

163

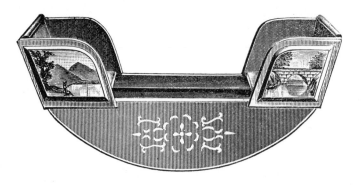 

C. W. F. Dare Chariots.

The Lover's chariot. Posed in it is the president of the Philadelphia Toboggan Company, Henry B. Auchy, in the front seat. This chariot is still used in Riverview Park, Chicago.

Columbia, the gem of Olympic Park, Maplewood, New Jersey and part of one of the finest and largest carousels in America. This rare chariot board, carved by Daniel C. Muller for the Philadelphia Toboggan Company, is part of an inside, smaller chariot, one of four on this beautiful carousel.

Roman chariot. Made by the Philadelphia Toboggan Company.

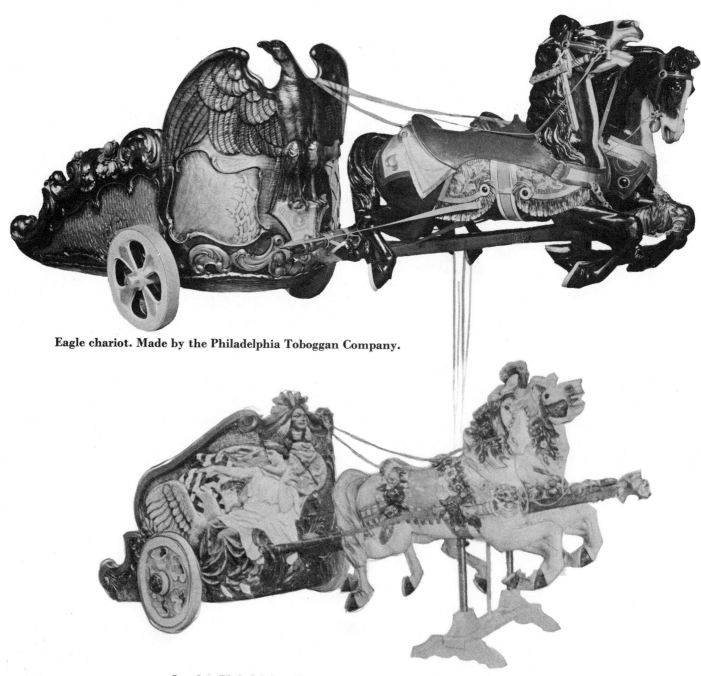

Eagle chariot. Made by the Philadelphia Toboggan Company.

On this Philadelphia Toboggan Company chariot, Columbia, in a pose influenced by Michaelangelo's "Creation of Adam," is bidding a mere feathered eagle to guard the path of the never-ending circle of carousel riders—while an Indian chief looks far into the distance.

Illions's dragon chariot

Parker chariot

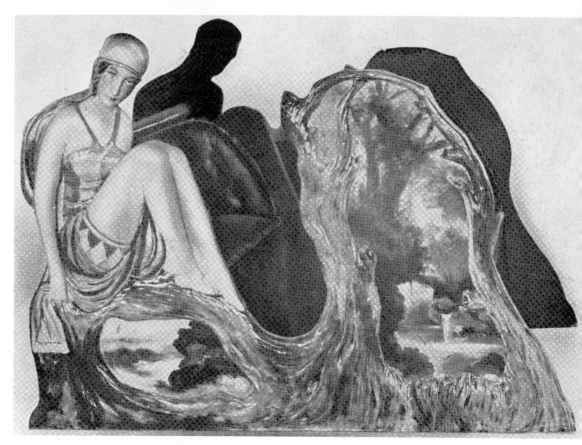

Herschell chariot featuring a carved and painted bathing beauty.

Whale car from a "Scenic Railway." Made by Orton Sons and Spooner Ltd.,
England. Each car seated ten passengers. (*William Keating*)

With the auto here to stay, this model replaced the chariot on German carousels made by Josef Hübner.

Lovers found more privacy in the shadows of this regal chariot with its cupid herald. Made by Josef Hübner.

Upper rim from the Olympic Park carousel. Made by Philadelphia Toboggan Company. It has 3,000 electric light sockets and a repeating patriotic theme.

Inside upper cornices of Olympic Park carousel.

Philadelphia Toboggan Company rim with a combination of Eastlake, Roccoco, and Italian Renaissance—plus panel paintings in the style of vaudeville drops of the 1915 period. The mirror hides the two joining sections of the rim.

Section of the carousel enclosure made by the Philadelphia Toboggan Company for the Los Angeles carousel.

Section of the outer rim from the author's Dentzel carousel in St. John Terrell's Music Circus at Lambertville, New Jersey. The mirrors are five feet wide.

Close-up of a section from the outer rim of the author's carousel

Section of a cornice with carved tassels, semi-circular oil paintings, and large colored-glass gems alternating with electric bulbs. Made by the Spillman Engineering Corporation.

Carved wooden shields from an unidentified carousel (George Breckner, Jr. Collection) once used to hide the joined sections of the rim.

A magnificent walkway and balustrade. The decorations were gold and scarlet with elaborate marbling effects. Painted panels of famed Venetian palaces and scenes from the Grand Canal completed the effects. Built by R. J. Lakin Company Ltd. for a "Ben Hur" ride. (*Eric Brown*)

Detail of the elaborate "Ben Hur" Lakin balustrade. (*Eric Brown*)

Carved center top from an unidentified English roundabout. (*Eric Brown*)

176

Rounding Board of Harvey's juvenile roundabout, 1920. (*Eric Brown*)

Rounding board of the "Grand Electric" galloping horses roundabout. (*Eric Brown*)

Since the application of steam to the carousel in 1865 by S. G. Soames of Marsham, England, the rapid development of the carousel was due to the various inventions and improvements in its machinery.

Gustav A. Dentzel was the first to apply steam to the carousel in the United States. The engine was directly geared by bevel gears to an upright shaft which communicated the power by direct gearing on the carousel. A small engine was also provided for the band organ which was driven by a belt from the main pulley. This came with boilers, fitting, and pipework.

Thirteen years after Soames's application of steam to roundabouts in England. C. W. F. Dare of Brooklyn, New York, supplied steam boilers, made by the New York Steam Power Company, to their carousels.

Lighting a carousel in 1878 was done by either the Wellington gasoline lamp with its gravity supply or the more elaborate brass suspension oil lamps. Lanterns and Dietz tubular square lamps were also used, burning kerosene, and were hung from nearby trees.

With the popularity of the Kiddie Park, and the rise in rent and real estate values, the operation of a huge park-type carousel has been found to be too costly and unprofitable. Operators find it more financially rewarding to install three and even four smaller rides in the same space that will gross many times the revenue of the larger machines.

Thus, many huge carousels have been dismantled, and broken up; their parts have found their way into antique shops, ended as lawn ornaments to rot away, become part of the current fad of bar stools. At this alarming rate, it will be just a matter of a few years before one of our greatest heritages will have disappeared from the American scene, except for those museums which have acquired whole carousels. The time has arrived when an organization, federally sponsored, should be created to record, preserve, and perpetuate this great phase of American life. The Henry Ford Museum at Dearborn and the Shelburne Museum in Vermont have complete carousels. More museums should follow this example or the merry-go-round may soon be extinct.

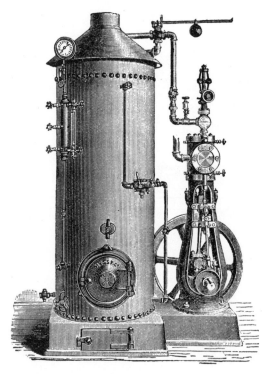

Steam boiler used by the C. W. F. Dare carousels

An advanced model Dentzel steam engine

The friction drive patented by Henry B. Auchy of the Philadelphia Toboggan Company and used on small carousels is still in use today.

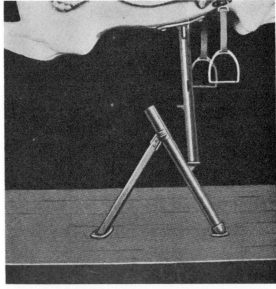

There were various types of effects for the up and down or jumping movement of the horses. An earlier model used by C. W. Parker was discarded for this model. Both got in the way of the riders and were shinscrapers.

The Allan Herschell 1916 horse pipe-telescope for jumping horses was far more practical and used the principle developed by Savage and improved upon by Mangels. The horse hanger (*right*) patented by Herschell in 1918 made rapid replacement and removal easier for carnival carousels playing short stands.

The inside drive of a portable Herschell ride shows the power, transmission, and the direct organ drive.

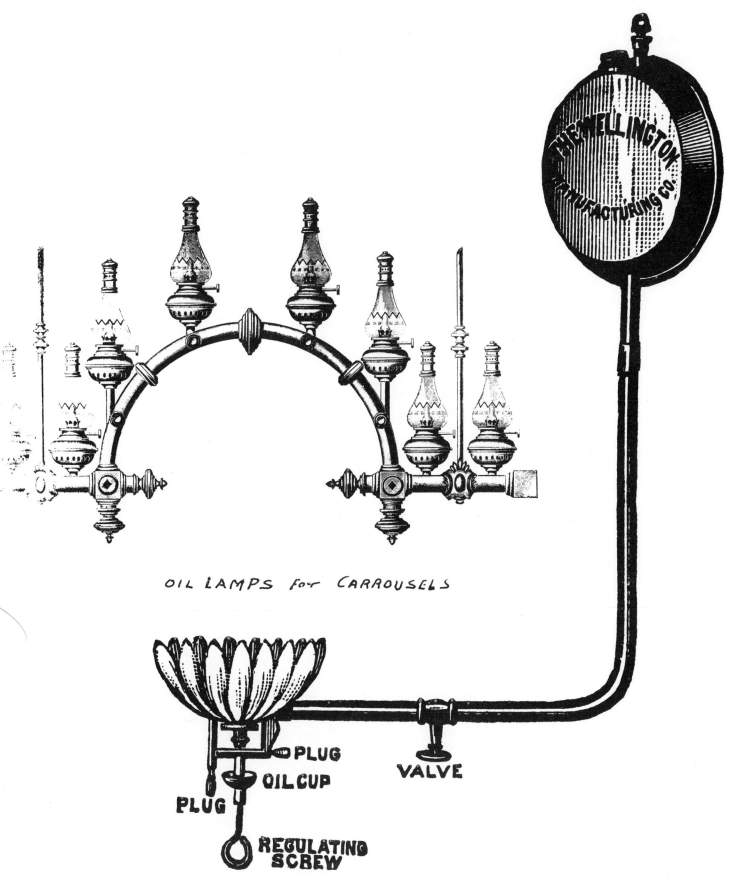

OIL LAMPS for CARROUSELS

PLUG

OIL CUP

PLUG

VALVE

REGULATING
SCREW

Carousel lamps

181

CHAPTER 6

THE BAND ORGAN AND
ITS MAKERS

THE MUSIC OF THE CAROUSEL IS AS EXCITING AS THE RIDE ITSELF. THE MEASURED RHYTHM, emphasized by the crash of cymbals and the beating of drums, makes the ride as irresistible as the piercing call of the steam calliope was for the circus parade.

The military band organ with its gaudy façade is as much a part of the carousel as the wooden horses upon its platform. The band organ, often called a calliope—mistakenly—is quite another instrument. The band organ with a great variety of shadings, pitches, and vocal tones has many virtuoso effects. (The calliope—pronounced *Kal-i-o-pee* but *Kally-ope* by circus folk—with its shrill, piercing notes, when played by steam or air, was meant to be heard at great distances to draw the throngs to the boat landing or Main Street for the circus parade.)

The band organ has an ancient ancestry. In the scriptures, it is recorded that Jubal, the son of Lamech, played on musical instruments before the deluge. He is called the "father of all such as handle the harp and organ." About 1 A.D., a hydraulic organ appeared on a Roman coin. About 130 years earlier, Hero of Alexandria, in his *Pneumatics* laid out a plan for a water organ—using the force of water as the turning power. Also, shepherds' and Pandean pipes as ancient instruments are well known.

By the twelfth century, the organ took the form sometimes seen in manuscript illustrations. In these, men on both sides pumped air, while in the center, the "musicians" manipulated the rudimentary controls.

Portable organs of the fifteenth century supplied air by hand bellows. The barrel organ in its simplest form was known as the "bird organ" which was designed to teach bullfinches to pipe. The bird organs played a simple melody. From 1657, this following method of laying out an organ cylinder was in use until the beginning of the twentieth century:

Transfer the Pythagorean melody to the aforesaid photactic cylinder. Since the melody consists of

182

Organ pictured on a Roman coin

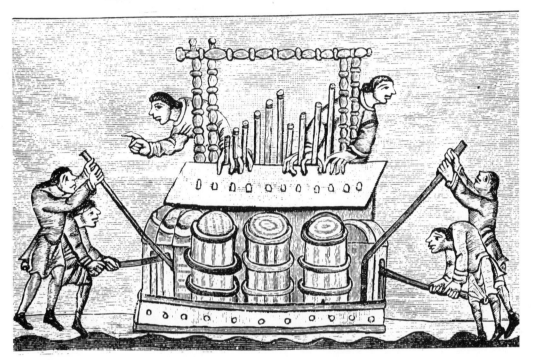

Organ from the twelfth century. (from a manuscript in Trinity College, Cambridge)

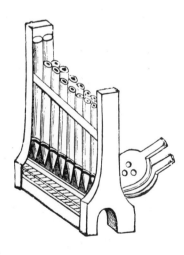

Portable organ from the fifteenth century

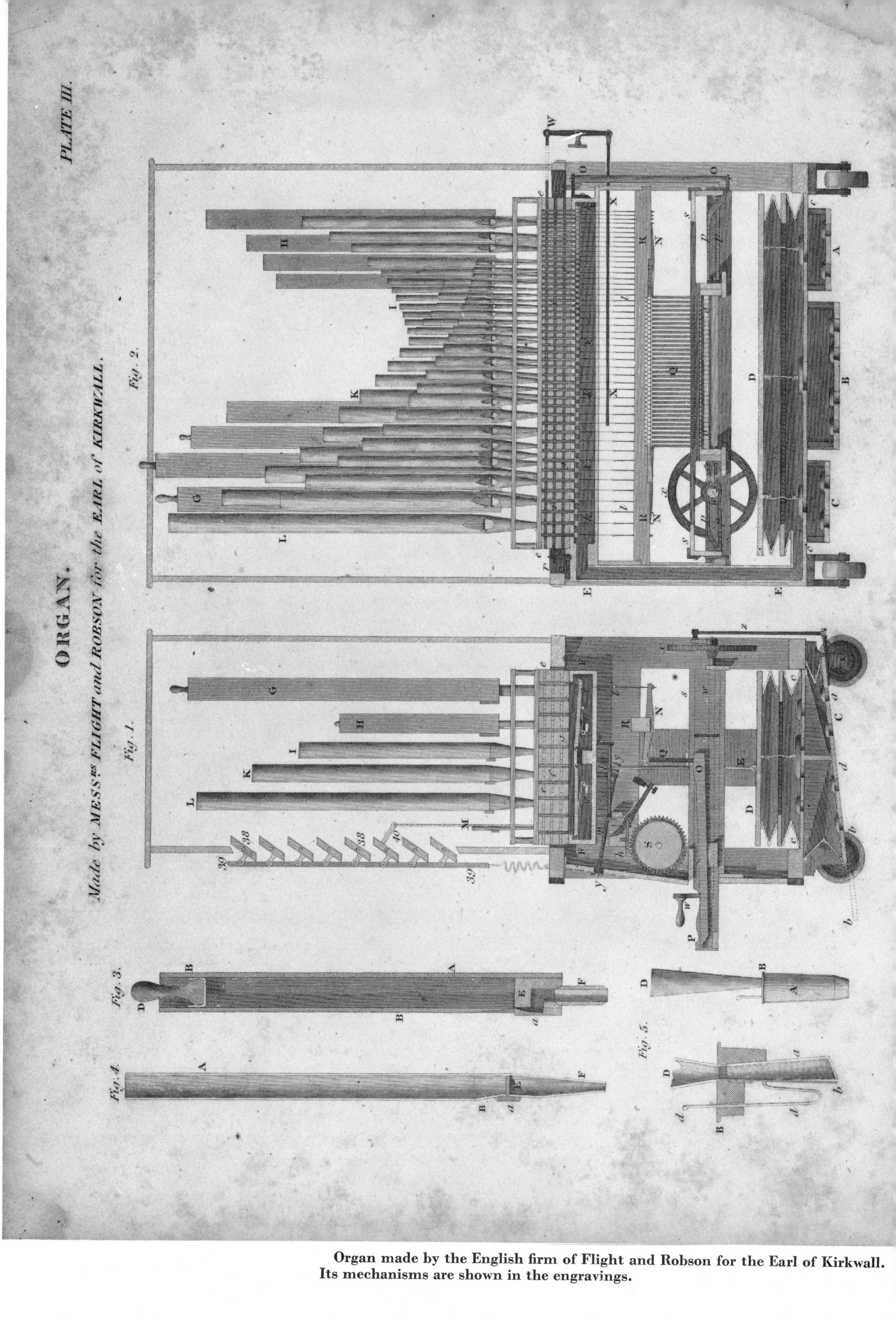

PLATE III.

ORGAN.

Made by MESS.ʳˢ FLIGHT and ROBSON for the EARL of KIRKWALL.

Fig. 1.

Fig. 2.

Fig. 3.

Fig. 4.

Fig. 5.

Organ made by the English firm of Flight and Robson for the Earl of Kirkwall.
Its mechanisms are shown in the engravings.

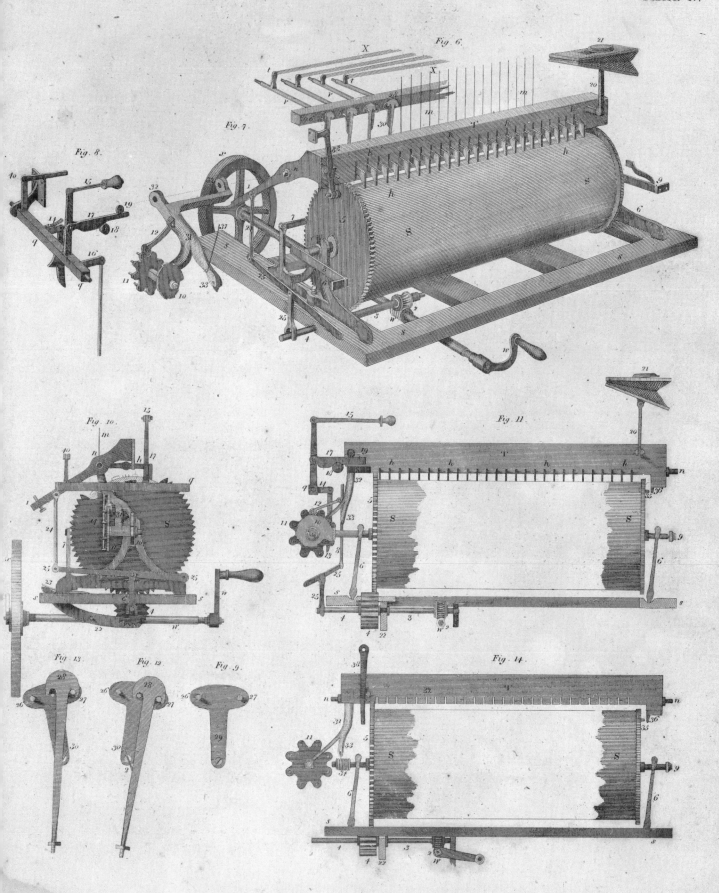

J. Farey Jun.r Del.

J. Bard fc.

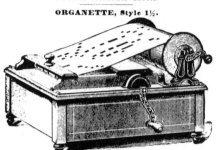
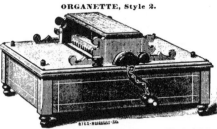
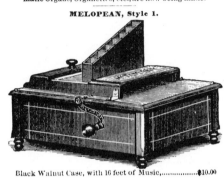

McTammany organettes

54 tunes or measures, the whole circumference of the cylinders should be divided into 54 equal parts; then each part should be subdivided into three parts since each note of this melody equals one-third of a measure. Heavy lines drawn longitudinally on the cylinder mark the melody and fix the teeth which correspond to the notes in the proper places.

The art of mechanical music and automata is as old as the art of fine clockmaking since a precise mechanism was needed to activate, relate, and sustain the complicated motions. The combination of a timing mechanism and a pinned or pegged cylinder could activate dancing dolls with several motions, turn the pinned cylinder, and turn itself off. Clock springs, weights, and hand power were all used to turn the organ barrel. The mechanization of the organ made it possible to develop the band organ as we know and hear it today.

The hand organ which turned a pinned cylinder or pegged wooden roller held only so many tunes. To change the tunes, new rollers were inserted. The size of the barrel limited the length of the tune and the number that could be used.

A great advance was made when the inventor of the silk loom, Joseph Marie Jacquard, a manufacturer of straw hats at Lyons, France, applied cardboard pages with perforations marking the patterns. Napoleon's attention was called to this inventive genius and a pension was granted Jacquard until his death in 1834.

In 1842, Claude Felix Seytre, also of Lyons, patented a similar perforated cardboard book for the automatic playing of musical instruments. In 1861, J. A. Teste made the first practical instrument using the perforated paper for organs and snare instruments. In America, a patent was granted to Hunt and Bradish of Warren, Ohio, for a small pianoforte controlled by a perforated paper roll. Meanwhile, the organ with a huge pegged wooden roller and a large number of pipes and percussion instruments came into use. Like the early carousels, its motive power was man or boy.

One of America's unrecognized geniuses, John McTammany, invented the "organette." His system, a forerunner of the modern piano roll, made the double-track band organ of

186

today possible. McTammany, poverty-stricken, could not pay the patent renewal fee or promote his invention; he saw it taken by others and successfully exploited. McTammany died penniless in 1915.

LUDOVIC GAVIOLI

The greatest of all band organ makers was Gavioli. Ludovic Gavioli, founder of the Société Gavioli et Cie brought his organ factory from Modena, Italy, to Paris, France, in 1845, realizing that this European metropolis was better situated to handle his very fine instruments. Gavioli was an expert organ builder with the highest standards of workmanship and artistic skills. His instruments were the best that could be made but the Gaviolis were not good business men. Ludovic turned over the administration of his business to his son, Claude. The firm's bookkeeper embezzled a great deal of money, forcing Ludovic to find new financial sources. This he did by taking into the business a Mr. Yver who had no organ experience.

The Gavioli organs were much in demand. One order came from Queen Isabella II of Spain who wanted an organ for her court chapel that automatically played religious music. In 1868, there was an uprising by the generals and the court had to flee, taking their organ with them, to Paris. The organ was sent to the Gavioli factory for an overhauling. In dismantling the organ, Anselme Gavioli found, hidden in the pipes, part of the crown jewels, unknown to the queen. The jewels were returned and after restoring the organ, Anselme and his young son Ludovic II, were presented at court.

Ludovic Gavioli (Drawn by Eugene Karlin)

Later, Anselme took charge of the factory with its many problems. In the war of 1870, the factory was moved to Alsace in eastern France. Much of the material was destroyed, forcing the Gaviolis to start all over again. Nevertheless, Anselme managed to bring the factory back to its flourishing level, mainly because of the success of his new organ inventions. Anselme worked hard, training specialists in organ building and pipe pitching.

About this time, the "harmonic brake" was invented which created a great improvement in the organ and its manufacture. However, the Gaviolis suffered a new reverse—one from which they never recovered. In 1901, the factory's foundation started to sag and a complete rebuilding was necessary. The expenses could not be met and specialists were laid off. One of these specialists, Charles Marenghi, who was their foreman for many years, and almost a member of the household, left the firm taking most of the best workmen with him. Marenghi, who knew all the Gavioli secrets of manufacture, put them to use in making very fine organs with grand façades. Marenghi died in 1919 and the business was continued for a few years by two of his workmen, the brothers Gaudin.

The final blow to Gavioli came when the administration of the business fell into the hands of men who were inexperienced in organ building. Various economies were tried, such as substituting paper for cardboard and using unseasoned lumber. Ludovic II, son of Anselme, tried to fight them and as a last straw, was forced to resign when the proud Gavioli name was used in making carpet sweepers—that didn't work. A similar fate was also to befall the great American music-box makers, the Regina Company of Rahway, New Jersey.

Of the innovations introduced by the Gaviolis, the most important was the book organ. Band organs were previously played by cylinders or rollers which were hand pinned—a laborious and expensive process. Up to 1910, American carousel makers were charging about $60 for a new roller, or a dollar a note. In 1892, Gavioli introduced the book organ; a series of perforated cardboard pages consecutively fastened to each other, which was fed through a pneumatic system, called the "Mechanical-Pneumatic Touch Key," which used the principles of the church organs.

THE DEVELOPMENT OF THE ORGAN

After 1892, the book organ was used on carousel and dance organs. No one thought they would replace the cylinder organs. But its success came not because of the quality of the music, but from the increased repertory and lowered cost. The number of keys of cylinder organs depended on the length of the cylinder. But the pneumatic book organ made possible greater ranges without increasing the size of the organ. The keys could be placed closer to each other than in the cylinder organ. By combining the book system and the pneumatics, it became possible to build a choice collection of different registers in the organs. Gavioli's invention was copied by many makers in France, then Germany and in Belgium.

Band organs are not all the same. There are different characteristics to the different kinds. There are dance organs, made expressly for dance halls and skating rinks. Carousel and fair ground organs and street organs. The dance organs accentuated the rhythm and were enormous in size, because of the large number of registers. Some reached thirty feet in height and twenty feet in width, taking up the whole wall of the dance hall. Carousel and fairground organs were stronger and higher pitched, with a penetrating sound in which the high registers carried the tune. In these organs one didn't hear the heavy chords accenting the rhythm, but the clear sound of the melodies.

German organs concentrated on trumpets, the French and Belgian on the baritone. To these, the Gaviolis and also the Gasparini added piccolos for a higher pitched effect, sometimes combined with a carillion built out of metal plates, called the "Metalofon." Some French and Belgian organ builders pitched their organs 1½ tones higher than Gavioli. The Germans maintained the C pitch, also differing from the French and Belgians.

Gavioli military band organ, 1875. (*W. J. Barlow*)

Grote-Gavioli organ (*W. J. Barlow*)

The street organs and these are mainly found in Holland, are more lyrical and sensitive in character. Amsterdam is the city of the street organ, called the *pierement*. Nowhere else in the world can one still see and hear as many as seven or eight in one group. These instruments are loved by the Amsterdammers and have become part of their way of life. During the day and evening, in the public squares, the *pierement* line up, playing singly or in a group the popular tunes, marches, waltzes, and modern hits. These instruments all have been endowed with names and representational scenes are painted on their heavily carved façades. The "Arab," the "Zaza," the "Jupiter," and others have their fans with the same enthusiasm as Americans for their ball clubs. The word *pierement* itself has its probable origin in the ancient Dutch word "*pieren*," to make music.

The street organs are placed on little carts and pulled about. They are all hand turned. Great pride and rivalry exist among these *pierement* people, and the instruments, mechanically and in appearance, are kept in perfect condition. About 1937, these organs were banned from

189

Typical barrel organ which can be found in any Dutch city. (*Frits Gerritsen*)

Marenghi 98-key organ, once part of Harry Hall's "Scenic Railway" at Derbyshire. (*Chiappa Ltd*)

the main part of the city. The ban was lifted in 1948 and twelve licenses were issued. Since cold and damp weather affects these instruments, April to August are the best months for their performances. In Amsterdam, in 1875, Leon Warnies, started street organ rentals and continued until his death in 1902. His widow continued the business. These street organs threw the itinerant street bands out of business and in turn were replaced by the phonograph and radio. The Warnies with a large number of expert tuners and repairers kept the instruments in perfect order.

Charles Marenghi continued in business making fine organs which became great favorites of English showmen. Many are still playing on roundabouts and English fairgrounds. Marenghi died in 1919 and the business was continued by the Gaudin Freres for only a short time after.

Limonaire Freres of Paris was founded in 1840 and made a fine line of organs. Limonaire took over what was left of the old Gavioli business, supplying their customers until their termination in 1918. Many Limonaire organs were sold in America with other, local names painted on the façade.

One of the lesser French organ makers, Alexandre Gasparini had been organized in 1865 and produced many fine organs. Part of the old Gasparini stock was brought to America in later years by Louis Berni, reconditioned and sold to the American carousel makers with his own name painted on the façade.

GERMAN ORGAN MAKERS AND OTHERS

In Germany, the two centers for band-organ manufacture were Waldkirch and North Berlin. In Waldkirch, the Bruder family and A. Ruth und Sohn had factories turning out large quantities of organs. In North Berlin, there were Frati and the firm, Cocchi, Bacigalupo und Graffigna—both of which were long established, making organs for steam circus, barrel organs, orchestrions, piano, and hand organs.

In Waldkirch, there were the Bruder Gebrüder, organized in 1806 by Ignaz Bruder; Ignaz Bruder Söhne, organized in 1876; Wilhelm Bruder Söhne organized in 1868 and Ruth und Sohn with Adolphe Ruth, the founder, who was still active near the turn of the century.

191

Perforating the Music Sheets by Machine.

Making the Bellows and Wind Chests.

Varnishing Organ Pipes and Finishing Embouchures.

Assembling the Batteries of Pipes.

The Back of a Small Orchestrion Opened for Adjustment of Certain Parts.

Carving and Decorating the Woodwork.

Setting Up the Front of a Large Orchestrion.

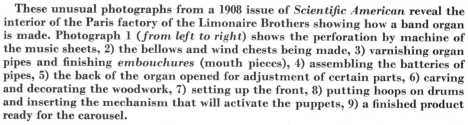

Putting Hoops on Drums and Inserting the Mechanism Into Puppets.

These unusual photographs from a 1908 issue of *Scientific American* reveal the interior of the Paris factory of the Limonaire Brothers showing how a band organ is made. Photograph 1 (*from left to right*) shows the perforation by machine of the music sheets, 2) the bellows and wind chests being made, 3) varnishing organ pipes and finishing *embouchures* (mouth pieces), 4) assembling the batteries of pipes, 5) the back of the organ opened for adjustment of certain parts, 6) carving and decorating the woodwork, 7) setting up the front, 8) putting hoops on drums and inserting the mechanism that will activate the puppets, 9) a finished product ready for the carousel.

Limonaire Orchestrophone

Limonaire Orchestrophone, 1903, with eighty-seven keys and the latest art *nouveau* façade. It has three figures—a band leader and two bell strikers—and sold for 9,900 francs.

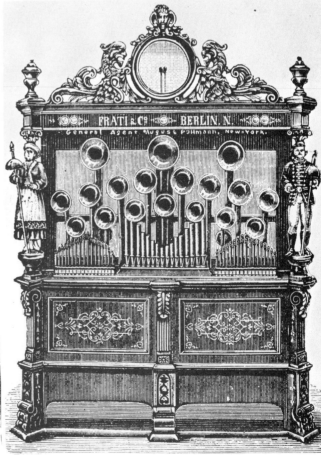

Frati organs, 116 and sixty-eight keys.

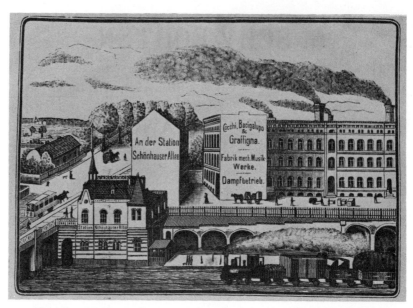

The Cocchi, Bacigalupo and Graffigna factory in North Berlin.

They all made very fine barrel organs but surprisingly few book organs even long after their intoduction by Gavioli.

One Frati organ was made for the American market in 1894 by their New York agent, August Pollman. It sold under the name of the "Auditorium Orchestrion," had 116 keys, twenty-four brass trumpets, ten brass bass trombones, bombardons, wooden trumpets, hautbois, clarionets, cornets, flutes, piccolos, double basses, etc. It had seven figures striking musical instruments, and had a cylinder containing ninety-six bars of music playing ten tunes of the most elegant and superb music. Price—an enormous amount of money for those days—was $11,000. An additional barrel playing ten tunes was an extra $600. Ringling Brothers Circus also bought a Pollman Frati organ with eighty keys, and extra wooden cylinders (serial number 6251).

The Cocchi, Bacigalupo & Graffigna made mainly small, hand-turned organs for street fairs and small carousels. In 1900, G. Bacigalupo, now in business by himself, at 79 Schonhauser Allee in North Berlin, issued a small catalogue with six models of portable organs of small dimensions.

In 1904, Louis Bacigalupi was brought to the United States by Gustav A. Dentzel to make cylinders for the carousel organs which he imported. Bacigalupi (having changed the "o" to an "i") did not stay long with Dentzel and opened his own shop, making cylinders and later his own system of rolls and roll cutting. He later moved to the West Coast and continued making organ parts and rolls. After his death, his business was carried on into the fourth generation by his son Louis, who made small organs for kiddie carousels.

In Waldkirch, A. Ruth und Sohn made fine organs of small and huge proportions. Many of each size came to America. The most ornate is now on the balcony at Steeplechase in Coney Island, Brooklyn, having arrived with the Hugo Haase "Eldorado" carousel before 1911. The organ is silent and hardly noticed, its glamor darkened by age. Another huge Ruth organ tours the United States with the Royal American Shows. The organ was kept in fine condition by A. L. (Tony) Crescio until his death in 1962.

Wilhelm Bruder Söhne made many organs which found their way to American carousels. Dentzel admired the tone and workmanship, using many on his carousels with his own name on the façade. Mangels preferred the large Bruder Gebrüder, placing one on the huge Feltman carousel in Coney Island.

Belgium produced some expert band organ makers who had a unified system of manufac-

Louis Bacigalupi

A. Ruth and Sohn organ. A mass of gold leaf and fine carving twenty-eight feet wide. The figure supporting the drum (*left*) may have originated in local folklore.

Hooghuys organ, eighty-seven keys. (*W. J. Barlow*)

ture, simplifying the interchange of rollers and other parts. This reduced expenses and costs, giving them a competitive advantage.

In Antwerp there were Emile Devreese, Th. Mortier, D. Daneels, and Pierre Verbeek. Aime Hooghuys of Brugge produced many fine organs with tones of excellent quality. This Hooghuys, with eighty-seven keys, using the Gavioli system, is part of the large collection at the private Fair Organ Museum in England, directed by W. J. Barlow.

AMERICAN BAND ORGAN MAKERS

In America, music as an accompaniment to the carousel was supplied in the early days by a drummer beating a tempo, sometimes joined by a flutist. A rustic band was uncommon. In the carousel that Dentzel used at Atlantic City, pulled by a horse with little Bill in a soapbox strapped on its side, the horse's harness covered with little bells provided the tonal effects. Mechanical music was available in New York City at the shop of Joseph Molinari on Elizabeth Street. Molinari was the supply for organ grinders and the owners of street pianos. His little factory turned out a large amount of hand organs and barrel pianos which he rented to hurdy-gurdy men throughout the East. The street piano was a common sight on the streets

American organ pioneers. Standing, Eugene DeKleist, George Herschell (*third and fourth from right*), James Armitage, Bert Stickney (*fourth from and extreme left*), Allan Herschell (*center*).

Rudolph Wurlitzer

of large cities and organ grinders with their performing monkeys were also abundant.

Molinari started his shop in New York during the Civil War, renting his products to itinerant street musicians, mainly Italians who had no trade. For sixty years, the Molinaris were in the same business, sometimes supplying instruments for small carousels. However, these were small, manually operated with a limited sound. Large organs had to be imported from Europe at great costs.

About 1890, the Tonawanda carousel-makers, who had been importing organs for their carousels, found that the new tariff laws made the import too expensive. Europe was searched for an expert who could build organs right in North Tonawanda. Eugene DeKleist was such a man. DeKleist was brought to America and began the manufacture of organs in Martinsville, which was later annexed to North Tonadanda. Armitage Herschell sold DeKleist a plot of land for one dollar upon which the organ factory and warehouse were built. DeKleist's firm, the North Tonawanda Barrel Organ Factory, was the first of its kind in America. His letter-head read, "Merry-go-round organs, military band organs, self-acting orchestrions, only manufacturers of the kind in the U.S." In 1891, the first organ was produced.

DeKleist who was born VonKleist in Dusseldorf in 1867 changed his name as representative, in Belgium and later London, for Limonaire Freres. In 1903, the barrel organ factory changed its name to the DeKleist Musical Instrument Company. DeKleist had approached the Wurlitzer Company. But, with many outlets for their instruments throughout the country, the Wurlitzers were not interested in selling band organs as the demand was not sufficient. They did commission DeKleist to make an electric piano with a coin attachment. Wurlitzer was selling coin-operated Regina Music Boxes and had built up a large business with them. DeKleist developed a ten-tune pin-cylinder piano called the "Tonophone." Wurlitzer had exclusive rights and promoted it with great success.

In the meantime, DeKleist was elected Mayor of North Tonawanda in 1907 and his office in City Hall was on property owned by Armitage Herschell. He neglected the Tonophone and was warned by Wurlitzer to either improve the quality or they would make it themselves or buy him out. In 1908, DeKleist agreed to sell his plant and Wurlitzer entered the manufacture of the military band organ.

Franz Rudolph Wurlitzer came to the United States in 1853 at the age of twenty-two, from Schoeneck, Germany. He went to Cincinnati, Ohio, selling goods from door to door. He found work as a porter and the following year got a job with a private banking firm at $8.00 per week. During his spare time, Rudolph observed that the music stores had a small stock which was overpriced. Wurlitzer's family, during the unproductive winter months, made fine hand-crafted musical instruments. He managed to save $700 and he sent it to his family with orders to send musical instruments. These he sold directly to the retailers—thus, informally, in 1856 the Rudolph Wurlitzer Company got its start. Wurlitzer engaged three rooms on the top floor of the Masonic Building in Cincinnati, carrying on the music business as a part-time activity, while still working at the bank as a cashier.

By 1861, he established a factory in Cincinnati, making military band instruments. By 1865, Wurlitzer was the largest outlet for band instruments in America and a retail store in Chicago was opened. By 1880, Wurlitzer designed a piano and had it made bearing his name. America was becoming music-minded; the periodicals all carried fine wood engravings showing all kinds of parlor instruments at low prices and competition for business was keen. America was entering the age of mechanical music.

Wurlitzer's three sons, Howard E., Rudolph H., and Farny R. Wurlitzer joined their father in his business. In 1904, a disastrous fire wiped out the Cincinnati headquarters. A new six-story building was built and remained their principal office until 1941 when the executive offices were moved to Chicago. The October 12, 1907, issue of *Billboard* carried the first advertisement for Wurlitzer military band organs. In 1909, Wurlitzer had seriously started the manufacture of band organs, producing a few styles designed mainly for skating rinks and carousels. With the use of a newly-patented roll mechanism, which rewound itself and started playing all over again, Wurlitzer organs were much in demand and the old roller organs were outmoded. Wurlitzer increased the styles and sizes of their organs and produced a notable group of fine organs for carousels, skating rinks, dance halls, etc. Many carousel operators found it cheaper to buy a new Wurlitzer than to have the old organs repaired or converted to paper rolls and many big fine old organs were junked. Some carousel operators were quite attached and loyal to their organs, found them louder and with finer quality but bought a small Wurlitzer as the second organ. By 1920, Wurlitzer organs were found in almost every park in the country.

By 1925, Wurlitzer had eighteen different models of band organs. By 1928, radio and the amplified phonograph replaced the music of the carousel organ. Wurlitzer discontinued their manufacture and the effects of the band organ division were sold to Ralph Tussing of the T. R. T. Manufacturing Company of North Tonawanda. Wurlitzer also made the following styles of organs: 20, 20A, 20C, 20D, 104, 105, 106, 130, 135, 140, 145B, 149, 155, 157, 160, 164, 165, and the Caliola.

The Wurlitzer, one of the truly native-made band organs, is a vanishing instrument; the few that are still in use are prized by their owners. Today, collectors are attempting to organize with a view to preserving one of America's happiest heritages. There is a group in the Musical Box Society International who are devoted to the restoration and preservation of these fine instruments.

In 1906, the North Tonawanda Musical Instrument Works was incorporated and a small factory was established at Payne Avenue at the Lockport Junction and Niagara Falls Trolly lines. They later produced a line of organs selling from $250 to $3,500. These "perfected military band organs came with pneumatic action, tracker board, starting and stopping mechanism and were operated by endless paper music."

Several of the styles offered, were undoubtedly of European manufacture, bearing a strong resemblance to the Waldkirch output. This firm made a large number of organs for all parts of the country.

The North Tonawanda Musical Instrument Works also made other mechanical instrumetns such as the Pianolin, Mando Piano Orchestrina—all were coin-operated. The firm was eventually taken over by the Remington Rand Company who continued producing organs into the 1920's.

Another maker of organs was the Niagara Musical Instrument Company at North Tonawanda whose production ran parallel with the North Tonawanda Musical Instrument Works.

The Artizan Factories, Inc. was at Erie Avenue and Division Streets in North Tonawanda with S. C. Woodruff as president. Besides organs and music rolls, they made orchestrions, pianos, player pianos and chimes. The double tracker system was used and seven styles of organs made. The largest size made at the factory in North Tonawanda was the Style "D" which had sixty-one keys. Artizan and Wurlitzer organs were used by The Spillman Engineering Corporation for their carousels.

In the lower part of Manhattan was a small group of organ makers whose production consisted mainly of piano organs, small cylinder carousel organs, and hand organs for organ grinders. Some of these, like Molinari, came from Italy in the second half of the nineteenth century.

Another New York organ maker was Ceasar Maserati of 92 New Chambers Street, who concentrated his labors mainly on the cylinder piano. These were mounted on carts and pulled about the city streets. Some were rented, others were bought on time payments. The sound of these street pianos is heard no more. A 1934 city ordinance forbid their use—except for two old men whose sole livelihood depended on their music-making; the last died in 1955.

Giovanni Mina came to America in 1880 and set up his organ business at No. 2 First Street in Manhattan. He also made cylinder pianos, cylinders for carousel organs, and some hand

Wurlitzer Merry-Go-Round Band Organ, Style 18
41 keys—music on pinned cylinders

Wurlitzer Military Band Organ, Style 103

Wurlitzer Rink or Carousel Military Band Organ, Style 125

Wurlitzer Band Organ, Style 146A

Wurlitzer Band Organ, Style 146B

Wurlitzer Band Organ, Style 148

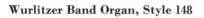

Wurlitzer Military Band, Style 150

Wurlitzer Duplex Orchestral Organ, Style 153

Wurlitzer Concert Band, Style 180 (Largest Wurlitzer carousel organ)

organs. His letters, written in flowery terms, indicate that he supplied rinks, merry-go-rounds and later, moving picture shows. G. Gazza succeeded Mina and moved to 71 Roosevelt Street, a short distance away, carrying on the business for just a short time.

Almost sixty percent of all organs imported to the United States came through the hands of Louis Berni. Perhaps no individual in the organ business had the influence and personality that Berni radiated. At the beginning of the century, Louis Berni came to the United States from Paris where his older brother had just taken over his father's business of organ renting. With several firms already established in this field, Berni found it rough going in New York. He decided to go after the carousel makers' business, introducing the new book organs. Berni took over a barn on Fifty-sixth Street in Manhattan and converted organs into the new paper-organ type. With his aggressive personality and considerable charm, he sold a great number of organs, helping him to open his factory at 219 West Nineteenth Street with a showroom on the other end of West Twentieth Street in Manhattan. Berni had an interest in the Auchy enterprises and supplied the Philadelphia Toboggan Company with organs for their carousels.

Berni made many trips to Europe and for some time represented the Gavioli factory in America. Louis Berni soon became known as the "Band Organ King" and some of the façades

A page from the Wurlitzer band organ catalogue showing style 165, designed for large carousels)

Wurlitzer, duplex roll mechanism made for continued, uninterrupted playing.

The North Tonawanda Musical Instrument Works

Models of the North Tonawanda Artizan Factories, Inc.

on his imported organs were more luxuriously carved than any Emperor's throne.

In 1909, Louis Berni encountered trouble in trying to buy band organs from his usual sources. Berni put on his derby and took the next ship to Europe. He found the opposition united and toured the remotest corners of the continent buying up any and all organs he could find, bringing them back to his New York factory for modernization. He inserted this ad in the March 13 issue of the *Billboard*. "Just arrived from Europe—large consignment with orders by the manufacturers to sell at cut-rate prices. 'We've got the trust beaten to a frazzle.' "

From time to time many obscure names appeared beneath the Berni façade and some of the towns were never heard of—baffling many a repair man. Some organs still turn up with the name of an odd organ maker—undoubtedly one of Berni's imports. He became quite wealthy and the story goes that when prohibition came in, Berni, who loved Italian wine, went out. Accounts of his activities in Europe were still being printed in *Billboard* during World War II.

Probably the most unusual organ ever made was the one especially designed for "General" Pisani by the B. A. B. Organ Company at 336 Water Street in Manhattan. The "General" originated a vaudeville act of playing tunes on the B.A.B. organ on the vaudeville stage by shooting .22 caliber bullets into it! It was made so that the scales and pipes were adjusted to the shooting. The bullets opened the valves and permitted the sounds to come out. The act was a hit in every sense of the word.

The B.A.B. Organ Company started in 1912 with Andrew Antoniazzi making street pianos. Borna joined Antoniazzi as a partner and added his experience to that of Antoniazzi who had worked for Maserati for six years. Later, Dominic Brugnolotti who worked for Molinari joined the firm and this able group converted a large number of cardboard organs to a new system of their own design of double-track paper rolls. Later they moved into the old Molinari factory in Brooklyn and made organs. Brugnolotti and Borna both died and Antoniazzi sold the remains of the factory to former Senator Charles Bovey of Virginia City.

About 1903, Charles Looff was supplied with organs by the Knapp Barrel Organ Works of South Howard Street in Philadelphia. Knapp made organs for a short time, competition forcing him to close.

One of the largest organs made and imported into America was handled by Ernst Böcker who came from Cologne, Germany. In a rare cylinder-maker's record book in the author's collection is a list of almost all the early organs, their locations, their makers, serial numbers, and the cylinders' scales. Such a record was necessary as all the many organ makers each

The Berni Organ Company

Gavioli organs at the Berni factory

Berni organ "superb"

B. A. B. Company organ

had a different scale system for their rollers. A 102 key Gavioli is recorded with a low serial number of 112 and was owned by Droge. Another Gavioli with ninety-two keys was on Morris's carousel at North Beach now LaGuardia Airport. Böcker had many accounts and his records show important customers throughout the East. The Colony Club-Ladies Dance Hall at Madison Avenue and Thirtieth Street had one of his organs, as did Sulzer's Harlem River Park at 127th Street and Second Avenue.

Anyone who has watched the carved organ figures leading the band, striking bells or drums has often been both amused and bewildered. The mechanical arrangement, synchronized to the music is actually very simple. The actions of these manikins created as much interest as the music itself. Sometimes, the mechanism becomes troublesome and the figures are taken off and discarded.

One museum among others that is preserving these old instruments and their capabilities of producing the original tunes and sounds is the fascinating Musical Museum at Deansboro, New York. One can actually play these instruments by dropping a small coin in the box. It s curator, Arthur H. Sanders, will patiently explain the history and origin of each instrument.

Long after the band organ music stops and the carousel unloads its passengers, flights of fantasy will continue, taking children to far-away story book places, fighting dragons on fiery steeds to the sound of heroic music. Many an adult reflects upon his youth remembering dreams long-forgotten. And though the world may be full of new ideas, new inventions, and great devices for making a better existence—no one will ever devise a greater or better object to give joy than the merry-go-round.

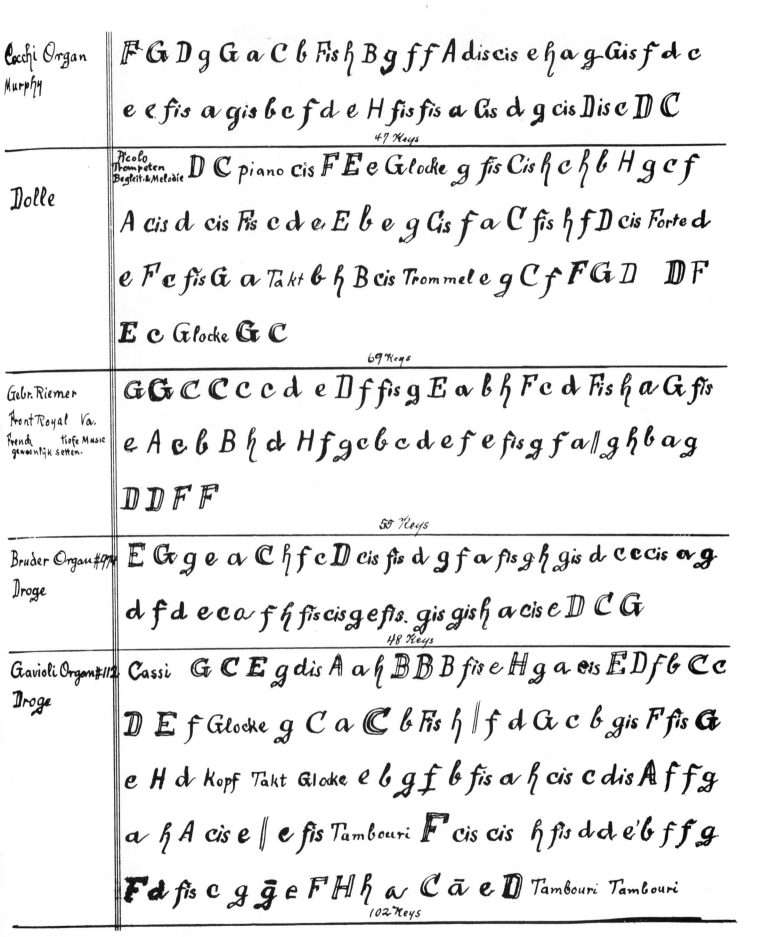

Cocchi Organ Murphy	F G D g G a C b Fis h B g ff A dis cis e h a g Gis f d c	
	e c fis a gis b c f d e H fis fis a Gis d g cis Dis c D C	
	47 Keys	
Dolle	Picolo Trompeten Begleit.&Melodie D C piano cis F E e Glocke g fis Cis h c h b H g c f	
	A cis d cis Fis c d e E b e g Cis f a C fis h f D cis Forte d	
	e F c fis G a Takt b h B cis Trommel e g C f F G D D F	
	E c Glocke G C	
	69 Keys	
Gebr. Riemer Front Royal Va. French tiefe Music gewoonlijk setten.	G G C C C c d e D f fis g E a b h F c d Fis h a G fis	
	e A c b B h d H f g c b c d e f e fis g f a ll g h b a g	
	D D F F	
	55 Keys	
Bruder Organ #97 Droge	E G g e a C h f c D cis fis d g f a fis g h gis d c e cis a g	
	d f d e c a f h fis cis g e fis. gis gis h a cis e D C G	
	48 Keys	
Gavioli Organ #112 Droge	Cassi G C E g dis A a h B B B fis e H g a e is E D f b C c	
	D E f Glocke g C a C b Fis h ll f d G c b gis F fis G	
	e H d Kopf Takt Glocke e b g f b fis a h cis c dis A f f g	
	a h A cis e ll e fis Tambouri F cis cis h fis d d e b f f g	
	F d fis c g g e F H h a C a e D Tambouri Tambouri	
	102 Keys	

Cylinder-maker's record book

Joseph Ch. Zima, one of the last great living carvers. He is seen here repairing a band organ figure.

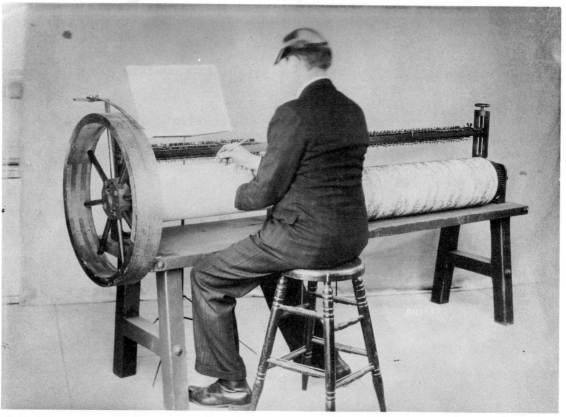

Cylinder-marking machine

Gavioli figure (Barlow Collection, England).

Gavioli figure. (*W. J. Barlow*)

The popular Wurlitzer at Deansboro Musical Museum, New York.

W. J. Barlow in his private organ museum adjusting arm of figure from Gavioli "Troubadour," designed and carved by the celebrated Ferdinando Demetz of Bolzano, Italy. (*W. J. Barlow*)

APPENDIXES

I. A CHRONOLOGICAL LIST OF GREAT AMUSEMENT-PARK FIRES

It is estimated by amusement ride insurers that fires and other forces of nature destroy at least two large park-type carousels each year. The author recently made an unofficial count of carousels still in existence and operating, and of the thousands once made, the total that remains is less than one hundred. Fire has been the demon of seaside resorts and amusement parks. The amount of damage in a quarter of a century is staggering. A chronological listing of these great fires follows:

1900	August 14	Chester Park, Cincinnati
1908	July	Coney Island, Brooklyn (almost completely destroyed)
1908	October 10	Wildwood Park, St. Paul, Minnesota
1908	December 2	Exposition Park, Conneaut Lake, Pennsylvania ($200,000 damage)
1911	May 29	Dreamland, Coney Island
1911	December 11	Luna Park, Coney Island
1913	September	Maple Beach Park, near Albany, New York
1916	May 9	Revere Beach, Massachusetts
1917	May 20	Woodside Park, Philadelphia
1917	November 29	Coney Island
1918	May 10	Coney Island, Cincinnati
1918	June 25	Forest Park, Chicago
1918	August 27	Revere Beach, Massachusetts
1919	April 30	Brighton Beach, Brooklyn (almost completely wiped out)
1921	December 21	Venice Pier, Venice, California
1923	March 29	Paragon Park at Nantasket Beach, Hull, Massachusetts
1923	July 18	Chester Park, Cincinnati
1924	January 6	Ocean Park, Venice, California
1924	September 26	Midland Beach, Staten Island, New York
1925	April 22	Saltair, Salt Lake City
1925	May 27	Electric Park, Kansas City
1927	October 11	Ocean City, New Jersey
1929	November 28	Paragon Park, Nantasket Beach, Hull, Massachusetts
1932	May	Central Park, between Allentown and Bethlehem, Pennsylvania
1932	July 13	Coney Island (most devastating conflagration in history of Coney Island)

Source: Compiled from the *Billboard*.

Park	Location
Alfarat	Altoona, Pennsylvania
Carnival	Kansas City, Kansas
Crystal Beach	Vermillion, Ohio
East Lake	Birmingham, Alabama
Erie Beach	Ontario, Canada
Flower Grove	Massachusetts
Fulton	Fulton, New York
Glenwood	Charleston, South Carolina
Highland	Massachusetts
Lagoon	Utah
Lake Wood	Mahanoy City, Pennsylvania
Lincoln	California
Mayflower Grove	Massachusetts
Neptune Beach	Niagara Falls, New York
Ocean Bay	California
Ocean City	New Jersey
Old Orchard Beach	Old Orchard, Maine
Prospect	Brooklyn, New York
River	Winnipeg, Manitoba, Canada
Rorick's Glen	Elmira, New York
Seattle	Seattle, Washington
Tashmoo	Detroit, Michigan
Terrapin	Parkersburg, West Virginia
White City	Chicago, Illinois

Spillman delivery records also show shipments to Liverpool, Le Havre, Naples, Baku, Tokyo, Manila, Singapore, Sydney, Cape Town, and other remote places.

Source: Compiled from Spillman catalogues and promotion material.

3. CARAVANS THAT FEATURED C. W. PARKER CARRY-US-ALLS

Aiken Amusement Company
Arena Amusement Company
Broadbeck Amusement Company
C. A. Bauscher United, Shows No. 1, 2, 3
C. W. Wortham, Shows No. 1, 2, 3
Con T. Kennedy
De Vaus
E. B. Reed
Ed A. Evans
George L. Layman Carnival Company
Johnny J. Jones Exposition
L. J. Eldred
Landes Brothers
Mighty Doris
Northwestern
Odus Mighty
Peerless Amusement Company
S. W. Brundage
Savidge Amusement Company
Southern Carnival Company
Tom W. Allen

Victoria
W. H. Forsythe
Wood Brothers
Yankee Robinson Circus

Source: Compiled from Parker catalogues and publications.

4. CAROUSELS BUILT BY THE PHILADELPHIA TOBOGGAN COMPANY

No.	Rows	Location
		1904
1	3	Norfolk, Va., then Manchester, N. H.
2	3	Topeka, Kansas
3	3	Columbus, Ohio
4	3	New Orleans, La.; then Manhattan Beach, Denver, Colo.; then Bergen Beach, Canarsie Shore, N. Y.
5	3	Milwaukee, Wisconsin
		1905
6	3	Elitches Garden, Denver, Colo.
7	3	St. Louis, then Jackson, Mich.
8	3	Ft. George, N. Y. (Amusement Co.)
9	3	Euclid Beach, Cleveland, Ohio; then Laurel Springs, Hartford, Conn. (Shop 1925— now #74R)
		1906
10	3	Richmond, Va., then Tulsa, Okla.
11	3	Willow Grove, Pa., then Cape May, N. J. (now #68R)
12	3	Chestnut Hill, Phila.; then Sea Breeze, Bridgeport, Conn.; then Crystal Beach, Ontario.
13	3	Hartford; then Broad Ripple, Ind.; then Bailey's Park, Norfolk, Va.; then Trier's West Swinney Park, Fort Wayne, Ind.
		1907
14	3	Bayonne, N. J.; then Classon Point, N. Y.; then South Beach, Staten Island, N. Y.
15	4	Ft. George, Wendell's Park; then Summit Beach, Akron, Ohio; to Milwaukee, Wis.
16	3	White City, Cleveland, Ohio; then Muncie, Ind.; then Puritas Springs Park, Cleveland, Ohio
		1908
17	5	Riverview Park, Chicago, Ill.
		1909
18	3	Louisville, Ky., then Worcester, Mass., then Erie, Pa. (now #78R)
		1910
19	4	Euclid Beach Park, Cleveland, Ohio
		1911
20	5	Ocean Park, Los Angeles, Calif. (completely destroyed by fire, 1912)

No.	Rows	Location
		1912
21	4	West Haven, Conn.; then Milford, Conn.; then Capital Park, Hartford, Conn.; then Savin Rock, West Haven
22	5	Asbury Park, N. J., then Atlantic City, N. J.
23	3	Pittsburgh, Pa.
24	3	Pittsburgh, Pa.
25	3	Pittsburgh, Pa.
		1913
26	3	Portable, sold to Joe Krouse. Zeidman, Greater Sheesley Shows;
27	3	Sold to Phila. Carrousel Co.; then A. K. Kline, Walt Shows
28		See 1914
29		See 1914
30	4	Mr. Spencer, Sydney, Australia
		1914
28	3	Portable, sold to Frank Herd, to Beckman, Gerety
29	3	Newburgh, N. Y. to Carsenia Park, Reading, then Port Arthur, Texas (1944)
30		See 1913
31		See 1915
32	3	Portable sold to Ralph W. Smith, N. Y. C.
33	4	Mr. McFadden, Minnesota State Fair Grounds, St. Paul
		1915
31	3	Lakeside Park, Dayton, Ohio
34	3	Portable, sold to Jos. C. Ferari, then Rubin & Cherry Shows
35	4	Luna Park, Cleveland, Ohio
36	3	Geo. W. Long, Rochester, N. Y.
37	3	Portable—in manufacture, see 1916
38	3	In manufacture, see 1916
		1916
37	3	Portable (Copping, Lusse)
38	3	Shellpot Park, Wilmington, Del.
39	4	Southeastern Fair Grounds, Atlanta, Ga.
		1917
40	3	Portable, sold to Johnny J. Jones (Lusse)
41	3	Ross Farms, moved to Wildwood, N. J. (Rhoads)
42	4	Fred Pearce, Detroit, Mich. (destroyed by fire)
43	3	Portable, sold to Wm. Glick; then to Pollacks
44	4	Riverside Park, Springfield, Mass., then, Roger Williams Park, Providence, R. I.
		1918
45	3	Cincinnati, Ohio (zoo)
46	5	Palace Gardens, Detroit, Mich., then Olympic Park, Maplewood, N. J.
		1919
47	4	Liberty Heights Park, Baltimore, Md.; then Auburn, N. Y.; then Hershey, Pa.
48	4	Ocean View, Virginia
49	3	Clementon, N. J.

No.	Rows	Location
		1920
50	3	Buckroe Beach, Va.
51	4	(In construction)
52	3	Frederick Road Park, Baltimore, Md.; then Wildwood, St. Paul, Minn., then Gwynn Oak Park, Baltimore, Md.
53	4	Central Park, Allentown, Pa.
54	3	Lincoln Park, New Bedford, Mass.
55R	3	Scranton, Pa. (old Allentown)

		1921
56	3	Meyers Lake Park, Canton, Ohio
57R	3	Flint Park, Flint, Mich. (burned, 1927)
58R	3	Merrimack Park (Buschman & Wehman), Seauga Lake, Ohio

		1922
59	3	Schuylkill Park, Pottsville, Pa.
60	3	Woodlawn Park, Trenton, N. J.
61	3	Idora Park, Youngstown, Ohio
62	3	Cumberland Park, Nashville, Tenn.; then Long Beach, Calif., 1941
63	3	Willow Grove Park (Built for Ocean Grove, N. J.), then St. Louis

		1923
64R	2	Wiest Amusement Company, Sunbury, Pa. Island Park
65	3	Riverview Park, Des Moines, Iowa; then Chattanooga, Tenn. (destroyed by fire)
66		See 1924
67	4	Evansville, Ind., Nehi Bottling Co.
68R	3	(Old #11) Cape May, N. J., then Coney Island, N. Y.

		1924
66	3	Luna Park, Schraft, Coney Island, N. Y.
69	3	McKeesport, Pa.
70	3	Belmont Park, Montreal, Canada

		1925
71	3	Shop 1925
72	3	Delaware Beach, Delaware Beach Corp. (jumper); then Waterbury, Conn.
73R	3	(Old McKeesport) Wildwood, N. J. (stationary)
74R	3	(Old #9)
75	3	See 1926
76	3	Excelsior, Minn.
77R	3	(From Valley Forge, Pa. Shop, 1925 Dentzel-made)
78R	3	(Old #18)

		1926
74R	3	(Old #9) Mt. Gretna, Pa.
75	3	Dallas, Pa.; then Rolling Green, Sunbury, Pa. 1944
77R	3	Valley Forge, York, Pa.
78R	3	(Old #18) Syracuse, N. Y.
79	3	Coney Island, Cincinnati, Ohio

		1927
63	3	St. Louis (from Willow Grove)

No.	Rows	Location
71	3	Jefferson Beach, Detroit, then Dayton, Ohio
80		See 1929
81R		See 1928
82R	3	Old Allentown, Pa., then Desmer's Beach

1928

No.	Rows	Location
81R	3	Rubin & Cherry Shows
51	4	Elitches Garden, Denver, Colorado
83		See 1931
84		See 1935
85	4	Nantasket Beach, Mass. (destroyed by fire)

1929

No.	Rows	Location
80	3	Mountain Park, Holyoke, Mass.
86R	3	Joyland, Lexington, Ky. (Old 74R)
73R	3	Lawnside, N. J. (stationary)

1930

No.	Rows	Location
71	3	Dayton, Ohio; then Walnut Beach
82	3	Atlantic City
87	3	In combination
88RA	3	Auburn; then Hook Mt.; then Rocky Glen Park, 1944
47	4	Baltimore; then Auburn

1931

No.	Rows	Location
83	3	Atlantic City; then Ligonier, Pittsburgh, Pa.

1932

No.	Rows	Location
87	3	Asbury Park, N. J.

1933

No.	Rows	Location
68R	3	Cape May, then Coney Island, N. Y.
60	3	Trenton; then Ocean City, N. J.

1934

No.	Rows	Location
38	3	Wilmington, Del., then Dorney Park, Allentown, Pa.
84	4	Old Orchard Beach, Maine
88RB	3	Lebanon to Wildwood, N. J. (destroyed by fire, 1944)
89R	3	Clementon, N. J., then Plum Island

Source: Compiled from the records of the Philadelphia Toboggan Company.

SOURCES AND READINGS

Beauvau, Louis de. *Fete et Carrousel*. Paris: Crapelet, 1828.

Beresford, J. *The Miseries of Human Life, or The Groans of Samuel Sensitive and Timothy Testy, With a Few Supplementary Sighs*. London: W. Miller, 1806–07.

Billboard, The. Billboard Publishing Co., Cincinnati. November 1894 to December 1949.

Boyer, Jacques. "The Manufacture of Mechanical Organs," *Scientific American*, April 4, 1908.

Bray, A. Watson. *Kiddielands, A Business With a Future*. Buffalo: Allan Herschell Co.

Brevets D'Inventions. Paris.

Brockhaus, F. A. *Auszug aus dem Konversations*. Leipsig, 1822.

Buchner, Alexander. *Mechanical Musical Instruments*. London: Batchworth Press.

Carey, David. *Life in Paris of Dick Wildlife* (*Whimsical Adventure of the Halibut Family*). Illustrated by David Cruickshank and John Fairburn. London, 1822.

Christenson, Erwin O. *Index of American Design*. New York: Macmillan, 1950.

———. *Early American Woodcarving*. Cleveland: World Publishing Co., 1952.

D'Allemagne, Henry René. *Récréations et Passe-Temps*. Paris: Hachette, 1905.

———. *Sports et Jeux D'adresse*. Paris: Hachette, 1903.

De Waard, R. *Van Speel Doos Tot Pierement*. Haarlem: Uitgeveru de Toots, 1962.

deWit, Paul. *Weltadressbuch der Musikinstrumenten Industrie*. Leipsig, 1893–1927.

Hamlin, John. *Flying Horses* (a novel based on the building of the first carousel in America). Philadelphia: J. B. Lippincott Co., 1942.

Hatch, Alden. *General Ike, A Biography of Dwight D. Eisenhower*. New York: Henry Holt and Co., 1944.

Havens, Catherine Elizabeth. *Diary of a Little Girl in Old New York, 1839*. New York: H. C. Brown.

Herzog, Sybil Jean. "Round and Round," *New York Times Magazine*, May 26, 1946.

History of Coney Island, A. New York: Burroughs and Co., 1904.

Hollowood, Bernard. "Toraquemada at Battersea," *Punch*, April 11, 1951.

Johnston, Richard. "The Carrousel," *Life*, August 27, 1951.

Jones, Barbara. *The Unsophisticated Arts*. London: Architectural Press, 1951.

Lambert, Margaret. *English Popular Art*. London and New York: B. T. Batsford Ltd., 1951.

Lee, Rose. "Noble Ancestry of the Carrousel," *New York Times Magazine*, September 24, 1924.

Leis, Gustav. "Der Komet," *Pirmasens*, 1912.

Lipman, Jean. *American Folk Arts in Wood, Metal and Stone*. New York: Pantheon, 1948.

Mangels, William F. *The Outdoor Amusement Industry*. New York: Vantage Press Inc., 1952.

Mellor, F. "Hugo Haase Visits London," *The World's Fair* (Oldham, England), January 30, 1932.

Menestrier, Claude François. *Traités des Tournou (Ioustes, Carrousels, Et Autres Spectacles Publics* Lyon: Chez Jacques Muguet, 1669.

Morley, Henry. *Memoirs of Bartholomew Fair*. London: Chapman and Hill, 1859.

Mundy, Peter. *The Travels of Peter Mundy in Europe and Asia, 1608–1667*. Printed for the Hakluyt Society, 1907–36.

Murphy, Thomas. "The Evolution of Amusement Machines," *Journal of the Royal Society of Arts*, No. 4855, Vol. XCIX, September 7, 1951.

New York Times Magazine. "A Visit to a Carousel Factory," March 19, 1899.

News of the Tonawandas, The. "Allan Herschell, Pioneer Business Man Is Dead," October 4, 1927.

Pilat, Oliver and Ranson, Jo. *Sodom by the Sea*. New York: Garden City Publishing Co., 1941.

Popular Science Monthly. "New Thrillers Defy Gravity," August 1927.

Pougin, Arthur. *Dictionaire Historique et Pittoresque du Theatre et des Arts Qui S'y Rattachent*. Paris: Librarie de Firmin Didot et Cie., 1885.

Roope, F. C. *Come to the Fair, The Story of the British Fairgrounds and the Showmen Who Attend Them*. Oldham, England: The World's Fair, 1961.

Stokes, I. N. *Iconography of Manhattan Island*. New York: R. H. Dodd, 1915.

Uzzell, R. S. "A Tribute to William H. Dentzel," *National Association of Amusement Parks Bulletin*, No. 4, Vol. 7, April 1, 1928.

United States Patent Office. Reports and Gazettes, 1797–1910.

Verdy, duVernois. *Recherches sur les Carrousels, Anciens et Modernes*. Paris: LeBrun, 1788.

Voltaire, Francoise Marie. *Siècle de Louis XIV*. Paris: Firmin Didot Freres, 1843.

5. LISTS OF PERSONNEL

Herschell-Spillman Carvers

Mr. Anderson

Mr. Bacon

Peter Flach

Herman C. Jagow

William Jagow

George Knack

Mr. Pasel

Bill Wendler

Allan Herschell and Spillman Engineering Corp. Carvers
Bert Bloomstine
Lloyd Bloomstine
Peter Flach
Fred Jagow
C. F. Kopp
Albert Lippich } Carved bodies for horses and worked on the larger animals from studio, 5250
Richard Lippich } Genessee Street, Bowmansville, N. Y.
Harry Nightingale
S. P. Paroski
Mr. Rubenburg
Bill Sprenger

Philadelphia Toboggan Company Carvers

F. H. Bensel
T. D. Bradshaw
A. Bruss
Albert Cardenti
Charles Carmel
Frank Carretta
Salvatore Cernigliaro
John Demian
William Euler
Joe Garelick
Jacob Krisavsky
Vincenzo Lanza
Frank Leone
David Lightfoot
Otto Melzar
Robert Morris
Alfred H. Muller

Daniel C. Muller
Henry Noz
Henry E. Richard
Salvatore Pat Russo
Joseph Tornatore
Louis Valenti
Dan Vecchiolli
John Zalar

MACHINE CARVERS
Carmine Chiarlanza
Charles J. Lorenz
C. J. Martin

SHAPED CENTERPOLES
Mr. Humes

Parker Employees

CARNIVAL
George Callahan
Chester Hutchinson
Con Kennedy (Parker's brother-in-law)

CARPENTERS
Mr. Gallagher
John Grove
Adam Gunzelman
William Gunzelman
Fred McCullough
Harvey Miller (foreman)
Abe Sauer
Harry Sauer
John Sauer

CARVERS
Joe Applegate (foreman)
Eugene Drisco
Phil Drisco
Lloyd Hutchinson
R. G. Shearer
Guy Tate
Loren White

FOUNDRY
Simon Barber
Red Bell
B. F. Freeman
Pete Hanneman

OFFICE
Ben Kessinger
Annette Tate
Emmett Tate
John Urie

PAINT SHOP
Tom Brown
George Dudley
John Filbreck
Tom Hogan

ORGAN SHOP
Christian Bath
Ted Bath
Clem M. Pleiser
William Priem

6. BAND ORGAN MANUFACTURERS

BELGIUM

Antwerp
  Bursens, J. 207 St. Berdsche Steenweg, Hoboken
  Daneels, Ferdinand 5 Greinstraat
  Koenigsberg, Ch. 32 Rue Huybrechts
  Mortier, Th. 56 Rue de Bréda
  Verbeek, Pierre 109 Duinstraat
Brugge
  Hooghuys, Aimé 56 Rue d'Ostende

BOHEMIA

Gall, Johann
Riemer, Gebr., Bernhard
Riemers, Joseph Sohne

ENGLAND

London
  Cleminti & Company, Cheapside
  Chiappa Ltd.

FRANCE

Paris
  Gavioli & Cie (A. Gavioli & P. Yver) 2 Avenue de Taillebourg
  Gasparini, Alexandre 11 et 18 rue de la Vega
  Limonaire Freres 166 Avenue Daumesnil
  Marenghi, Charles (Dir. Alexandre Cayron) 12 Avenue de Taillebourg

GERMANY

Berlin
  Asmus, Emil 23 Levetzostr., Berlin N.W. 87
  Cocchi, Bacigalupo & Graffigna, Schonhauser Allee 78, Berlin N.
  Fratti & Co.
Dresden
  Kaufman & Sohne, Ostraallee 19,
Waldkirch
  Bruder, Gebrüder
  Bruder Söhne, Ignatz
  Bruder Söhne, Wilhelm
  Ruth & Sohn, A.

ITALY

Airola
  Abate, Giuseppe
Alessandria
  Pastore, Frederico
Bari
  Petruzelli, N. Strada Palazzo di citta, 24
Bitonto
  Cuonzo, Vincenzo
Bologna
  Simoni, Gaetano, Via Rialto 13-2
Cremona
  Pozzi & Figlio, Giuseppe, Via Felice Geronimi 11
Genoa
  Campora Fratelli, Vico Orti San Andrea 32

ITALY

Milano

Foglia, Carlo, Via Olocati 37,
Pinerolo (Torino
  Falcone, Felice
  Viora, Michele
Roma
  Bianchetti, Augusto, Via Cavour 206
  Marazzi, Achille, Piazza della Chiesa Nuova 26
  Martini-Scialanti, Carlotta, Piazza dell Esquilino 18,
  Moneta, Riccardo, Via della Consolazione 112
  Scialanti, Alessandro, Piazza Principessa Margherita 161
Vezzano Ligure
  Giangrandi, Antonio

NETHERLANDS
Amsterdam
  Hilboeren, John Leliegracht 50
  Van Leeuwen & Zoon P. Nieuwendijik 211
  Warnies, Ludwig Brouwersgracht 214

POLAND
Warsaw
  Szymanski & Sohn, Chlodna 34,

RUSSIA
St. Petersburg
  Kornilow, J. K. Jekatarinski Kanal 67,

SWEDEN
Upsala
  Anstrand, J. G. Bafvernsgrand 19.

UNITED STATES
New Jersey
  Glen Rock
  Muzzio Organ Works, 237 Hamilton Avenue
New York
  Brooklyn, New York City
  Firmbach & Son, Joseph, 373 South 2nd Street
  George Messig, 742 Gravesend Avenue
  Molinari & Sons, G., 112 32nd Street
  B.A.B. Organ Company 112 32nd Street
  Manhattan, New York City
  Berni Organ Company, 111 W. 20th Street
  Boecker, Ernst, 432 East 17th Street
  Gravano & Zarrella, 229 Park Row
  Mina, Giovanni, 229 Elizabeth Street
  Maserati, Caesar, 92 New Chambers Street
  Molinari & Sons, 153 Elizabeth Street
  Muzzio & Son, John, 178 Park Row
  North Tonawanda
  Artizan Factories, Inc., Erie Avenue & Division Street
  North Tonawanda Barrel Organ Company, Eugene de Kleist
  North Tonawanda Musical Instrument Company, Payne Avenue
  Rudolph Wurlitzer Company
Pennsylvania
  Philadelphia
  Knapp Barrel Organ Works, 1407 S. Howard Street

INDEX

ACKNOWLEDGMENTS

THE AUTHOR EXPRESSES HIS GRATITUDE TO THE MANY INDIVIDUALS AND ORGANIZATIONS WHO have contributed information and material making possible the realization of this book. Also, to Fred and William Mangels, Jr. for permitting me to use the Mangels's library; to my English friends for their wonderful cooperation, and especially to W. J. Barlow of the Fair Organ Museum; to Eric Brown for his photos and Thomas Murphy for the use of his historic data on English amusement machines. I am also indebted to Salvatore Cernigliaro for the use of his carver's sketchbook and his autobiography; to my brother, Jack Fried, (my West Coast assistant) who has tirelessly aided me in this work; to William H. Dentzel who has furnished me with valuable information and photos of his family's history and business; to Romana Javitz, Curator of the Picture Collection, New York Public Library, who has guided me in my search for illustrative material, and to the owners of amusement parks throughout the country for their cooperation. Finally, to my wife Mary Hill Fried for her patience, encouragement, and painstaking assistance with translations.

The author also thanks the following: John C. Allen, A. Antoniazzi, Oneta M. Baker, G. P. Barnes, Seth Barter, Jr., Joseph L. Carrolo, J. H. Chandler, Richard Geist, Stephen L. Gilman, Rev. Father P. R. Greville, R. C. Illions, Allan Herschell Company, Roy L. Herschell, Mabel Jagow, Barbara Jones, Ted Kostew, R. J. Lakin, Clarence O. Lewis, David H. Logan, Ray Lusse, Thomas E. McCary, F. Mellor, Adam L. Moore, Constance Baker Motley, Ward R. Olver, James J. Onorato, Harvey Roehl, Royal Society of Arts, Arthur H. Sanders, Savages Ltd., Philip Seskin, Arthur R. Simmons, Swen Swenson, *Architectural Review*, "The World's Fair," Farny R. Wurlitzer.